SAN FRANCISCO *& The Bay Area*

"BAY AREA ENTERPRISES"
BY RICHARD DEFENDORF

WINDSOR PUBLICATIONS, INC.
CHATSWORTH, CALIFORNIA

SAN FRANCISCO *& The Bay Area*

ART GARCIA

MARTY OLMSTEAD

JOHN K. WATERS

SAN FRANCISCO & THE BAY AREA
California's Golden Gateway to the Future

By Art Garcia, Marty Olmstead and John K. Waters

Managing Editor: Linda J. Hreno
Senior Editor: Teri Davis Greenberg
Editor, Profiles: Jeffrey Reeves
Profiles Coordinator: Kelly Goulding
Assistant Profiles Coordinator: Keith Martin
Associate Editors, Profiles: Michael Nalick, Kevin Taylor
Proofreaders: Martha Cheresh, Lin Schonberger
Researcher: Ann Marie Taylor
Editorial Assistant, Profiles: Kimberly J. Pelletier
Consulting Editor: Mary Kirby

Designer: Christina L. Rosepapa
Photo Editors: Robin L. Sterling, Larry Molmud
Production Associate: Jeffrey Scott Hayes
Art Production: Amanda J. Howard

Copyright © 1992 Windsor Publications, Inc.
All rights reserved.
Published in the United States of America, 1992
by Windsor Publications, Inc.,
21827 Nordhoff Street,
Chatsworth, CA 91311,
with the support of CCA, Inc.
Elliot Martin, *Chairman of the Board and CEO*
J. Kelley Younger, *Publisher and Editor-in-Chief*
Nellie Scott, *Sales Manager*
Terry Pender, *Controller*
Printed in Hong Kong

Library of Congress Cataloging-in-Publication Data

Garcia, Art, 1935-
San Fransisco & The Bay Area : California gateway to
the future/by Art Garcia, Marty Olmstead, and John
K. Waters. p. 216 cm. 25x31
Includes a chapter titled: Bay Area enterprises/by
Richard Defendorf.
ISBN 0-89781-443-6
1. San Francisco Bay Area (Calif.)—Civilization. 2. San
Francisco Bay Area (Calif.)—Description and
travel—Views. 3. San Francisco Bay Area (Calif.)—Eco-
nomic conditions. 4. San Francisco Bay Area
(Calif.)—Industries. I. Olmstead, Marty. II. Waters,
John K. III. Title. IV. Title: San Fransisco and the Bay
Area.
F868.S156G37 1992 91-42109
979.4'61—dc20 CIP

TITLE SPREAD: This sweeping vista of San Francisco and the East Bay was taken from the vantage point of Diamond Heights. Photo by Kerrick James/The Photo File

THIS PAGE: San Jose's annual Cinco de Mayo parade is just one of many diverse ethnic cultural celebrations that characterize the Bay Area's wide range of international influences. Photo by Gerald L. French/The Photo File

CONTENTS

7

8

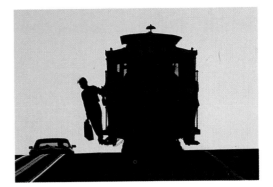

9

10

11

12

With San Francisco as its hub, the Bay Area is truly a magnificent metropolis. Photo by Tom Vano/The Photo File

HAVEN OF OPPORTUNITY, HOME OF CHOICE

By Art Garcia

he San Francisco Bay Area, America's fourth-largest metropolitan area, is home to six million people living in 96 cities, including the cosmopolitan, world-class city of San Francisco. The nine counties that make up the region include San Francisco (officially referred to as the City and County of San Francisco), Alameda, Contra Costa, Marin, Napa, San Mateo, Santa Clara, Solano and Sonoma.

The waterside community of Tiburon in Marin County is a great place for weekend brunch. Photo by Lee Foster/ The Photo File

❑ ❑ ❑

▲ THE CITY OF SAN FRANCISCO

San Francisco, crown jewel and focal point of the Bay Area, is the region's leading financial and administrative center, the site of numerous international corporate headquarters, a major player in Pacific Rim trade, the location of 64 foreign consulates, the Port of San Francisco, and international tourist and trade offices. This city/county, offers a wealth of cultural and recreational resources, magnificent architecture, fine restaurants and unsurpassed shopping opportunities.

San Francisco is a city for the senses—the fog drifts in from the Pacific; foghorns croak their notes of caution; cable car bells clang the joy of sliding up and down hills; street musicians play tunes on corners and in plazas; the aroma of sourdough bread, cappuccino, fresh-cooked crab, spices from a Chinatown restaurant or garlic from an Italian counterpart wafts through the air; stalls brimming with colorful flowers dot corners of Union Square's upscale shopping area and hot dog and pretzel vendors satisfy the tastes of those on the go—all part of the unique ambience that has made the city an international tourist center that hosts more than 13 million visitors a year.

Universal and cosmopolitan, the city is an experience, a mind-set, "everybody's favorite city." Former French president Georges Pompidou once said, "Of all the cities in the United States, (San Francisco) is the one whose name conjures up the most visions and more than any other incites one to dream."

Paul Erdman, international economist, former banker and author of best-selling novels about business and intrigue, maintains an apartment in downtown San Francisco as well as a 20-acre cattle ranch 50 miles north in the Dry Creek Valley of Sonoma County.

For Erdman and his family, San Francisco combines physical beauty with all the elements of an international city, much like Paris. In comparing the two, Erdman notes:

"One great advantage San Francisco has over Paris is that if you want to go to the Riviera from Paris, for example, or to the Alps, that's a long trip. But in the Bay Area, we're surrounded by rivieras in Monterey, Carmel and Pebble Beach and it's only a few hours to the Sierra Nevada Mountains at Lake Tahoe or Yosemite. If you want to go to Provence from Paris, it's an all day journey, whereas, to go to our "Provence" is only an hour to the wine country of the Napa and Sonoma valleys. What makes San Francisco unique is that it's a small, beautiful, cosmopolitan city in the middle of all of these alternative areas that provides everything you want within a few hours."

San Francisco's Fisherman's Wharf fills the senses with sights, sounds and mouthwatering aromas. Photo by Ed Young/The Photo File

▲ BAY AREA COUNTIES

Many people are also choosing to settle down in Alameda County, making it the region's second most populous county (after Santa Clara County) and California's sixth most heavily populated county (with about 1.3 million residents). It is the location of some of the fastest-growing communities in the Bay Area, including Oakland (the leading city of the East Bay), Berkeley (one of America's most politically adventurous and culturally diverse communities), Emeryville (home of Biotech Alley), Alameda, San Leandro, Castro Valley, Hayward, Newark, Fremont, Pleasanton and Livermore. In addition, Alameda is the region's most diverse-looking county, displaying a varied geography of wooded hills, white-wine vineyards, streams, lakes and the thriving Port of Oakland.

Contra Costa County seems to have everything—a growing business community, miles of countryside, cultural and recreational opportunities, outstanding schools and a modern transportation system. The county faces San Francisco and San Pablo bays on the west and adjoins the Carquinez Strait and the San Joaquin River Delta on the north. Once a collection of bedroom communities for other Bay Area urban centers, the county now draws city dwellers seeking a touch of suburbia and newcomers looking for a semblance of small-town living. Among the county's cities and towns are Concord (a rapidly growing city in

the eastern part of the county), Walnut Creek (Contra Costa's financial hub and a services center for the East Bay), San Ramon (home of a huge business park), and the residential communities of Orinda, Diablo, Concord, Pleasant Hill, Danville and Blackhawk.

Marin County, almost surrounded by the Pacific Ocean and bays and tethered to San Francisco by the Golden Gate Bridge, offers a breathtaking landscape of mountains (topped by majestic Mount Tamalpais), redwood forests, coastal areas and wooded hills. It has shared in the Bay Area's growth through a steady transition from bedroom community for workers in San Francisco to its own

Oakland, the heart of the East Bay, has its own vital downtown and charming residential neighborhoods complete with Victorian architecture. Photo by Gerald L. French/The Photo File

Contra Costa County, which comprises part of the East Bay, was once known primarily as a collection of bedroom communities. Now, however, the county has its own thriving business community as well as its own cultural and educational institutions. Photo by Bob Rowan/Progressive Image

The San Pablo Dam
Reservoir in Contra Costa
County is one of many
county recreational spots
providing a scenic retreat
for residents. Photo by
Bob Rowan/Progressive
Image

business, commercial and retail center with the
lowest unemployment level of all the Bay Area
counties (by the end of the 1980s) and population
growth remains below that of the rest of the region
due to high average home costs, scarcity of
available land and an above average cost of living.
About one-third of Marin's total land area has
been set aside for parks and open space preserves.
Among the county's communities are San Rafael
(its oldest and largest city), Sausalito (a picturesque
retreat for artists, writers and craftspeople, many of
whom live aboard houseboats moored along the
waterfront), Bolinas (a quiet colony whose
residents value their privacy), San Anselmo (North-

ern California's antique capital), Inverness, Toma-
les, Tiburon, Belvedere, Mill Valley, Larkspur and
fast-growing Novato, which is predicted to lead the
county in population and job growth between
1990 and 2005.

Napa County, often referred to as Napa Valley,
is the heart of California's wine industry with more
than 160 wineries. The Napa Valley Viticultural
Area stretches 30 miles north from San Pablo Bay
to the foot of Mount St. Helena and the Mayaca-
mas Range to the west and the shores of Lake
Berryessa on the east. Tourism flourishes here and
the area ranks as the sixth most popular destination
of vacationing Californians and the seventh most

popular among out-of-state visitors. Tourists take winery tours and hot-air balloon rides, go soaring in gliders, immerse themselves in Calistoga mud baths, enjoy fine dining and shop. The county has rapidly expanding service and retail sectors, and its competitive wages are especially appealing to small manufacturers. Though the least densely populated of the North Bay counties, Napa is projected to see the greatest population and job growth. Napa, St. Helena, Calistoga, Yountville, Angwin, Rutherford and Kenwood are among the county's towns.

San Mateo County boasts a diversified economy, one of California's lowest unemployment rates, 45 miles of scenic coastline and beautiful beaches and an ideal climate, making it a great place to live and work. The county is also a popular convention spot and home to the Cow Palace, San Mateo Expo Center, and Circle Star Theater as well as San Francisco International Airport. With the state's third-largest per capita income, San Mateo County is Northern California's sixth-largest market and con-

tains five regional shopping malls. The cities of San Mateo, Menlo Park, Foster City, San Carlos, Redwood City, Atherton, East Palo Alto, North Fair Oaks, Belmont, Burlingame, Hillsborough, Millbrae, San Bruno, South San Francisco, Daly City, Woodside, Portola Valley, Pacifica and Half Moon Bay all fall within the county's boundaries.

Santa Clara County, the region's economic powerhouse, is home to a highly educated and entrepreneurial population and about 3,000 high-tech companies in Silicon Valley (the research and development center for the electronics industry). Half of Northern California's most profitable companies are located here as are a strong venture capital community and major educational and research institutions (Stanford University, Stanford Linear Accelerator Center, NASA/Ames Aerospace Center). With rich cultural and recreational resources, the county is also a fine place to live as well as make a living. Among the communities of Santa Clara County are San Jose (California's first capital, the nation's 12th-largest city and the state's third

A community well known for its artists, Sausalito lies north of San Francisco with the two connected by the Golden Gate Bridge. Photo by George Hall/The Photo File

FACING PAGE: San Mateo County boasts 45 miles of scenic coastline. The lighthouse at Pigeon Point is seen here. Photo by Dave Porter/The Photo File

ABOVE AND TOP: The Napa Valley Wine Train, which runs through Napa County, celebrates the area's tradition of fine wine-making. Photos by Mark E. Gibson

largest), Milpitas, Mountain View, Palo Alto, Los Altos, Santa Clara, Sunnyvale, Cupertino, Campbell, Saratoga, Cambrian Park and Alum Rock.

Solano County, the region's fastest-growing county, is located halfway between San Francisco and Sacramento. Its population grew by more than 33 percent in the 1980s. With a comparatively large supply of affordable land for housing and commercial development, Northern California's largest port-oriented industrial park, the University of California at Davis campus and some unique recreational offerings, the growth will most probably continue. Benicia, Fairfield, Vacaville and Vallejo are some of Solano County's communities.

Sonoma County, located to the west of Napa County, possesses a landscape that is a study in contrast. Grazing sheep roam the hillsides along the rocky coastline, while vineyards and apple orchards blanket the valleys. Dozens of wineries are contained within the county borders. The county's population tripled between 1950 and 1980, with almost half the growth occurring through the 1970s and an 11 percent increase in the first five years of the 1980s. It is estimated that by 2005 the population will increase by 154,000, a 46 percent increase from its 1985 population. The county's economy is diversifying as manufacturing grows and tourism, lumbering and agriculture become less important to the overall economy. Among the county's towns are Santa Rosa (the rapidly growing county seat), Petaluma, Healdsburg, Bodega Bay, Sebastopol, Sonoma, Cloverdale, Geyserville, Rohnert Park, Cotati, Guerneville and Glen Ellen. A few miles from downtown Sonoma are country roads leading to towering redwood forests, the Russian River, pastured hills, mountain ridges, the ocean and the Valley of the Moon.

▲ The People

The Bay Area is also a home of choice for one of the world's most heterogeneous populations that represents 20 percent of California's population (with another one million people projected to settle in the area over the next two decades.) Indeed California's and the San Francisco Bay Area's ethnic diversity is strikingly different than that of the rest of the nation. The 1990 Census counted 12.5 million Hispanic, Asian and black Californians among the state's 30 million residents (more than 40 percent of the U.S. total). According to the Center for the Continuing Study of the California Economy in Palo Alto, more than 2 million immi-

grants came to California in the 1980s, and they and their children accounted for half of the state's population growth.

The latest U.S. Census found California maintaining its diversity and rapid growth, a state the Center describes as becoming less, not more, like its neighbors. "California is the new melting pot of America," says Stephen Levy, director of the Center, and the Bay Area plays a big part in making the pot boil. By the end of the 1990s, ethnic minorities will make up half the state's population, work force and consumer market, according to Center projections.

More than half of all refugees to the U.S. are from Southeast Asia, and California receives almost half of total U.S. refugees. The Bay Area receives more than 20 percent of Southeast Asian refugees, a disproportionate number for its size. According to the U.S. Immigration and Naturalization Service, the Bay Area is third overall in foreign immigration, following New York City and Los Angeles-Long Beach. The population mix of the Bay Area now is 65 percent white, 15 percent Asian, 12 percent Hispanic and eight percent black.

BELOW: California and the Bay Area lead the nation in foreign immigration. It is estimated that by the end of the twentieth century ethnic minorities will comprise half of the state's population. Photo by Chromosohm/Sohm

San Francisco residents celebrated the 50th anniversary of the Golden Gate Bridge in 1987. The bridge was closed to automobile traffic for the celebration, allowing 800,000 pedestrian revelers to enjoy a spectacular scenic view. Photo by Chromosohm/Sohm

The baroque architecture and detailed painting of these old Victorian homes, some of which predate the Great Earthquake of 1906, provide a unique living tribute to the city's history. Photos by Kerrick James

Home construction is on the rise as more people discover the benefits of life in the San Francisco Bay Area. Photo by Mark E. Gibson

Foster City typifies the urbanization and strong economic growth of San Mateo County. The county boasts California's third-largest per capita income and Northern California's sixth-largest market. Photo by Mark E. Gibson

▲ QUALITY OF LIFE

For decades the region has been synonymous with an enviable quality of life, despite its comparatively high cost of living. According to a joint report by PG&E and the Greenbelt Alliance (an environmental land-use group), "the Bay Area has kept its native born residents and attracted dynamic people and enterprises from around the world with its beautiful climate and environment, robust economy and vibrant sense of community."

One Bay Area resident who cherishes the region's quality of life is Shirley Nelson, chairman, chief executive, and founder of Summit Bank in Oakland. She stated enthusiastically:

I love the Bay Area. It's like living everywhere at once, all within an hour. I've done a lot of traveling, mostly in Europe, and every place I go, I find there's nothing out there that we don't have here. Everything, from the theater and restaurants to the mountains and the ocean, is within an hour or two.

Bay Area residents also prefer the region's moderate climate and diversity of landscape. Throughout the region a wide spectrum of natural and manmade environments can be found, from forested Mount Tamalpais in Marin County and rugged Mount Diablo in Contra Costa County to thousands of miles of waterway that flow into the bay through the delta's twists and turns from

Sacramento, from Oakland's downtown Lake Merritt and Jack London's Waterfront to the sweeping
panoramas from Grizzly Peak above Berkeley and
the pristine backcountry along the coasts of San
Mateo and Santa Cruz counties.

Maintaining the region's natural beauty and
high quality of life is a concern shared by the people of the Bay Area. Public opinion polls show that
local residents still believe the Bay Area is a good
place to live; they're just worried about how long
the life-style they love will last.

The Bay Area has been a forerunner in the state
and a model for the rest of the nation in its regional planning approach to handle the issues of over-
crowded roads, air pollution, water quality and

affordable housing. Even as its new frontier spirit
drives the Bay Area to the forefront of advances in
computer technology, aerospace and biomedicine,
its protective sense of history prevents change from
completing a major makeover of the area.

Issues ranging from transportation to air-quality
control are addressed on a regional basis and dealt
with through regional planning, perhaps more so
than in any other major metropolitan area in the
country. In addition, private or quasi-public
groups—the Association of Bay Area Govern-
ments, the Bay Vision 2020 Commission, and San
Francisco 2000—are lobbying for and leading
growth planning to develop a blueprint for the
region's future.

**Highway 1, with its
twists, curves and
coastal vistas, leads the
traveler through Northern
California. Spectacular
scenery and vibrant com-
munities make the Bay
Area an unparalleled
place to live. Pictured
here is Devil's Slide in
San Mateo County. Photo
by George Hall/The
Photo File**

▲ CREATIVE HAVEN

Many people have chosen to remain in or relocate to the Bay Area because of its numerous economic opportunities and its reputation as the "world's laboratory for ideas." For example, the East Bay counties of Contra Costa and Alameda contain a mix of prosperous industries that includes manufacturing, service and high-tech firms. South from San Francisco, Silicon Valley begins in San Mateo and stretches through Santa Clara County. Palo Alto is the northern reach of what a San Francisco Chamber of Commerce Bay Area business report calls "this high tech mecca." And the southern nexus is San Jose, from which rapidly growing high-tech companies are spreading outward and eastward to Fremont, Pleasanton and Livermore in southern Alameda County.

With the University of California at Berkeley in the East Bay and Stanford University in Palo Alto (35 miles down the peninsula), the Bay Area has also become a spawning ground for innovations and breakthroughs in science, medicine and technology. These campuses, with their worldwide academic reputations, have been influencing how the world lives, builds and does business for decades. From the birth of the cyclotron at Berkeley and the transistor at Palo Alto to the microchip in Silicon Valley and bioscientific assaults on mankind's deadliest diseases in San Francisco and across the bay along "Biotech Alley" (the bridge-to-bridge stretch from Richmond south to Hayward), the Bay Area has lived up to its billing as the "world's laboratory for ideas." San Francisco Economic Development Corporation President Kent Sims states that in the San Francisco Bay Area "creativity is about putting things together. We celebrate that."

FACING PAGE: Fireworks explode in a burst of color over the Oakland Bay Bridge, illuminating the waters of the San Francisco Bay. Photo by Kerrick James

Berkeley and San Francisco came to be most closely associated with the counterculture movement of the 1960s and today they remain havens for political activism and cultural diversity. Photo by Chromosohm/Sohm

PLAYGROUND ON THE BAY

by Marty Olmstead

Ask any 100 residents what they like most about living in the Bay Area and you'll get 100 different lists of answers. At the top of just about everyone's, however, is the region's delightful climate that lends itself to an array of outdoor recreational activities. The weather is so temperate that it's never too cold for a bike ride and never too hot to play golf.

Many people attracted to the Bay Area tend to be active, demanding as

The bracing northern Pacific air and unspoiled coastline of Ocean Beach and other seaside locations provide a natural refuge from big-city life for those who like to jog or walk along the beach. Photo by Kerrick James

❏ ❏ ❏

much from their outdoor environment as from their cultural milieu. For all their sophistication, many Bay Area residents like nothing better than spending a day at the beach or aboard a sailboat.

San Francisco and its eight neighboring counties all have some kind of shoreline along the 558-square-mile bay. The best water access, however, can be found either in the city itself or in Marin County, where Sausalito, Tiburon and Belvedere are all boating communities. Along the waterfront are private yacht clubs and public marinas as well as historic ships to tour.

With two major rivers and several small ones as well as creeks and sloughs all bringing fresh water into the ocean and bay, San Francisco Bay is able to support abundant marine life. The region's famed sea lions, which can be heard barking on the rocks off the Cliff House, and the harbor seals seen cavorting around Fisherman's Wharf are frequently joined by other seagoing mammals, including the occasional humpback whale.

In the bay itself are dozens of species of fish, ranging from small sharks to tiny herrings that provide an abundant catch during the winter.

The entire bay is on the flyway, which provides excellent birdwatching. Besides the everpresent seagulls, geese, hawks and falcons can also be seen.

The opening of yachting season in early April heralds a long summer of sailing on the breezy waters of the bay, but one doesn't need to be a boat owner to join the fun. It's possible to rent boats, kayaks and windsurfers, especially in Sausalito. This small scenic town boasts another unusual attraction: seaplane rides and lessons. One of the best possible ways to get one's own bird's-eye view of the entire region is from a small plane.

One of the most romantic activities in the Bay Area is a bay cruise. In addition to charter fleets that go out for regular dinner cruises as well as for private parties, there are working ferries.

FACING PAGE: The sun slowly sets over the boating community of Sausalito in Marin County. Photo by Mark Snyder/The Photo File

LEFT AND ABOVE: San Francisco Bay supports an abundant variety of marine life, including sea lions, seals and elephant seals. The Farallon Islands National Wildlife Refuge offers a safe haven for many of these aquatic mammals. Scarlet, the elephant seal pictured here, appears relaxed and content. Photos by Mark E. Gibson

Regularly scheduled service is offered daily between San Francisco and Larkspur, Sausalito and Tiburon in Marin County and between the city and Vallejo in the East Bay. Thousands of commuters choose this relaxing form of transportation to get to their jobs and back home again. On weekends the ferries are more likely to be crowded with families and tourists loaded up with cameras, eager to take home film memories of the sweeping skyline and the dramatic sight of Angel and Alcatraz islands.

Alcatraz Island, the notorious federal penitentiary that came to be called The Rock, is accessible daily via the Red & White Fleet ferries. The two-hour trip includes a guided tour describing the intriguing history of this isolated facility, which was closed as a prison in 1963 and is now overseen by the Golden Gate National Recreation Area (GGNRA).

For something more lighthearted, there's neighboring Angel Island State Park with its hiking trails and picnic sites. From the 781-foot summit of Mount Livermore, there's a 360-degree view of the island, the bay, and the surrounding terrain. Thick with wildflowers in the spring, Angel Island is also home to raccoons and deer. The island's history, though fascinating, is not as well known as that of Alcatraz. Ayala Cove was once a quarantine station where arriving travelers, seamen and immigrants had to wait out the incubation period for various diseases. There is Civil War history here as well and visitors can tour the old parade ground and, on weekends, visit a restored home that once housed officers' families.

But one needn't leave terra firma to hike along San Francisco Bay. The three miles from the Golden Gate Promenade east of Fort Point all the way to the Marina Green provide some of the most scenic jogging and hiking trails anywhere. There's a sandy beach in front of Crissy Field and on the huge green itself, weekends find families walking, picnicking, flying kites and playing frisbee. A relatively new attraction here is the wave organ, an innovative sculpture that allows the bay's waves to provide truly organic music.

BELOW: Alcatraz Island is famous for the "escape-proof" federal penitentiary that once housed many of the nation's most notorious criminals. Tours of the island and former penitentiary rank high on the must-see lists of visitors to the Bay Area. Photo by Mark E. Gibson

RIGHT: Sailing on San Francisco Bay is one of the many outdoor recreational opportunities enjoyed by Bay Area yachtsmen. Depending on the weather, one might see a lone sailboat or a veritable fleet out on the bay. Photo by Kerrick James

▲ PARKS AND RECREATION

A demand for public recreational facilities has resulted in an extensive park system within each Bay Area county as well as in a number of national and state parks and attractions. In addition to its open land and athletic facilities, the Bay Area features numerous other types of attractions such as wildlife preserves and amusement parks.

The city of San Francisco boasts more acres of parkland per capita than any other American town. The queen of them all, of course, is the famous Golden Gate Park, 1,017 acres of lakes, waterfalls, streams, hills, glades, forests, gardens and meadows. Once inside this entrancing oasis, it's hard to believe the entire area was once merely sand dunes that stretched inland from the ocean.

Visitors are probably first lured to the park by reports of the exhibitions at its prestigious museums, or perhaps by word of the fantastic displays at the California Academy of Science. Probably

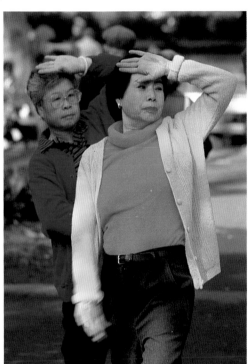

every San Franciscan, however, has a favorite outdoor spot in the park. The excellent tennis courts are in constant demand, but there is also room for baseball, soccer, football, jogging, roller skating, soccer, rugby, archery and rowing. Polo, which once was played regularly here, is making a comeback. And the park is also home to a number of foot and bicycle races. (Several shops nearby rent skates or bicycles or both.)

Within the park are the Golden Gate Stables, which offer riding lessons on park trails. There is a field for playing the French game of petanque and model yacht enthusiasts sail their craft on their own lake. For maps and information and a bit of history about this masterpiece, a stop at the McLaren Lodge near the Stanyan Street entrance to the park is essential.

Golden Gate Park offers quiet pleasures besides sports activities. The gardens are lovely year round; it's always nice to stroll through the

LEFT AND ABOVE: Chinese-Americans practice *t'ai chi* in North Beach's Washington Square Park. The Bay Area has one of the world's most ethnically diverse populations, with 65 percent of the population anglo, 15 percent Asian, 12 percent Hispanic, and eight percent African-American. Photos by Chromosohm/ Sohm

Strybing Arboretum, for instance, with its creek, pond and special botanical collections. At the northwest corner is a footpath known as the Redwood Trail, which leads through a veritable outdoor classroom of more than 100 plants.

Stow Lake, an artificial body of water best known for pleasant rowing, also offers an enchanting walking path around its rim.

On Sundays most of the park's streets are closed to automobile traffic, and cyclists and skaters rule the road. An excellent bike route is the 7.5-mile stretch from the Fell Street side (east) of the park down South Drive to Sunset Boulevard and on out to Lake Merced. Another option is to pedal all the way out to the beach and cruise along the Great Highway.

Lake Merced is not as well known as Fisherman's Wharf, but it is also an excellent spot to fish. You won't find any salmon or rock cod, but freshwater trout is the catch of the day during season. A reserve reservoir south of San Francisco Zoo, Lake Merced has a restaurant, bar, some picnic areas, and a boathouse with rowboats, canoes and pedal boats for rent.

Some people find the nine-hole course in Golden Gate Park a bit breezy for their tastes (and their handicaps). Nearby is another choice, Lincoln Park Golf Course. The oldest 18-hole course in the city, its scenic terrain also affords

some excellent vistas of the Golden Gate Bridge.

The San Francisco Recreation and Parks Department is an invaluable source for information on public recreational facilities, including more than 100 city tennis courts. Most are available free of charge, though there is a fee after 5 p.m. at the Golden Gate Park courts (which can be reserved on weekends).

West of Golden Gate Park lies the Pacific, which is fronted by a four-mile strand known as Ocean Beach. While few folks like swimming here, it's a marvelous place for walks, picnics, beachcombing and surfing or surf-gazing.

On the north side of the Cliff House, Lands End, one of San Francisco's legendary points of interest, can be reached by steep trails down dangerous cliffs. A picnic area lies at West Fort Miley near the public golf course at Lincoln Park.

Two other San Francisco beaches can be found closer to the Golden Gate. China Beach is so secluded that many locals even overlook it. Baker Beach, slightly east, offers stunning views of the Golden Gate Bridge and the Marin Headlands across the gate. Picnic areas come with barbecue grills in the slopes up from the beach near El

LEFT: Stinson and Rock-away beaches are two favorite spots for Bay Area surfers. Photo by Chromosohm/ Sohm

FACING PAGE TOP: Located in the Marina district of San Francisco, the Palace of Fine Arts houses the Exploratorium, a hands-on, interactive, science museum. Photo by Mark E. Gibson

BELOW: Baker Beach is a favorite place to fish, swim and surf. Photo by Gerald L. French/The Photo File

Named after the pioneering naturalist John Muir, Muir Woods in Marin County attracts thousands of visitors annually. Photo by Gerald L. French/The Photo File

It is the largest urban park in the world. Within it are some 100 miles of trails, picnic spots, beaches and redwood forests.

Visible from all over the Bay Area, Mount Tam (as it is affectionately known) symbolizes all that Marin has to offer. Near the Pan Toll Ranger Station is the Mountain Theater, a lovely amphitheater where musicals are produced each summer. From here a good hike can take half a day or more, depending on the route. The skyline of San Francisco is visible from dozens of vantage points on the eastern and southern slopes.

The most famous spot here is Muir Woods, a fern-lined grove of ancient redwoods that draws thousands of tourists year round. There are larger redwoods to the north, but a 252-foot-tall tree is still an inspiring sight, and many of the ones in Muir Woods are several hundreds of years old.

Of the three routes "over the hill" to the seashore, the favorite for first-timers is the coastal one, Highway One. Muir Beach, the first settlement on the coast north of San Francisco, is a tiny enclave flanking a small but stunning beach. It is a favorite stop for cyclists who crowd the roads here every weekend.

Better for swimming is Stinson Beach, a much larger town to the north. Here are a state park, a number of shops and restaurants, and the mouth of the Bolinas Lagoon. The abundant waters of this protected lagoon attract both resident and migratory birds. The best place to take a pair of binoculars is Audubon Canyon Ranch, a couple of miles north of Stinson on Highway One. Egrets and great blue herons are spotted in large numbers during the spring and summer months, when they return from their migrations for the breeding season. A half-mile trail leads from the parking lot to Henderson Overlook, where it is easy to observe bird behavior at close range.

Highway One continues on its inland path north to the town of Olema, gateway to the Point Reyes National Seashore. The jewel in the GGNRA's crown, this 65,000-acre wonderland seems lost in time. There are villages such as Inverness as well as grazing land for cattle, but most of this treasured parcel remains as Mother Nature intended. From chaparral and moors to grassy hillsides and pine forests, from salt marshes to a jagged shoreline of seemingly endless beaches, Point Reyes epitomizes the grandeur of the California coastal region.

Camino Del Mar. There are swimming and surfing here as well as fishing for striped bass and perch.

Located due north of San Francisco across the Golden Gate Bridge is the scenic county of Marin, which beckons with thousands of undeveloped acres of national, state, county, and local parks. From the seashore to the 2,600-foot peak of Mount Tamalpais, Marin is a mecca for outdoor enthusiasts. Windsurfing, swimming, bicycling, hiking, horseback riding, wildflower walking and birdwatching are only a few of the recreational opportunities.

The Golden Gate Recreation Area comprises 39,000 acres in Marin and San Francisco counties.

The Bear Valley Visitor Center dispenses maps, information and permits to camp in any of four sites. Nearby a recreated Miwok Indian village shows how the peninsula's original inhabitants lived and thrived in times past.

Visitors have their choice of myriad hiking trails of varying difficulty and some of the park can be toured on rental horses. But much can be seen from the comfort of an automobile along paved roads that lead to places such as Drake's Beach, ideal for picnicking and beachcombing. Point Reyes Beach is a wind-strewn 10-mile stretch of sand near the tip of the peninsula, and numerous other beaches lie hidden, awaiting the adventurous explorer.

Not to be missed is the the cliff-side Point Reyes Lighthouse. On foggy days a tour of the structure will suffice. In clear weather the site offers unparalleled vistas of the Pacific and between mid-December and early April, the best location for sighting the magnificent gray whales that pass close to shore on their annual migrations between Alaska and Baja California.

ABOVE: Mount Wittenberg in Point Reyes provides excellent hiking with views of grassy hillsides, pine forests and the jagged shoreline of Point Reyes National Seashore. Photo by Mark E. Gibson

LEFT: Many of the world's finest fishing locations, such as the Seal Rock Cliff House off of Point Lobos, can be found along the Northern California coast. Photo by Amy Seidman-Tighe

In Sonoma County, across the county line from Marin, the coastal road leads through a number of small towns with casual restaurants specializing in local seafood. In Bodega Bay it is possible to charter private fishing boats, but on rough days it is best to leave the work to the professionals. North of Jenner, Highway One hugs the oceanfront cliffs, offering one of the most breathtaking rides anywhere.

Jenner is at the mouth of the Russian River, which wends its way across Sonoma to the ocean. Along the way are resort towns backed by redwood forests and overlooking riverside beaches. Rafting, canoeing, swimming, fishing and kayaking are some of the summertime diversions in this traditional rural retreat.

East of Santa Rosa are a number of parks, including the sprawling Sugarloaf Ridge State Park and Annadel State Park, both with more than their share of scenic hiking trails and picnic facilities.

During the winter months there are guided horseback trips through Sugarloaf. In the summer the horses are available at neighboring Jack London State Park, which is also home to a museum devoted to the legendary author's life and works.

The town of Sonoma boasts a four-mile bike path that leads west from the downtown area. Nearby is Sonoma Train Town, a pint-sized version of a steam train that makes its way through forested acres past waterfalls and ponds and stops at a small petting zoo deep in the woods.

East of Sonoma County, Napa County has become synonymous with world-class premium winemaking, but there is more to recommend a visit than just wine tasting.

For an overview of the luscious Napa Valley, the best bet is a sunrise flight in a hot-air balloon. A number of companies offer these excursions, which last a couple of hours and usually culminate with

FACING PAGE: Sitting at the tip of Point Reyes National Seashore in the Golden Gate National Recreational Area, the landmark Point Reyes Lighthouse offers a panoramic view of the Pacific. Photo by Gerald L. French/The Photo File

ABOVE: Sonoma County's charm is due in large part to its small towns and older buildings. The Sonoma Hotel on Spain Street in the town of Sonoma is characteristic of the area. Photo by Patty Salkeld

LEFT: The coastal region of Sonoma County is enhanced by quaint Bodega Bay, the site of Alfred Hitchcock's film *The Birds*. The building used as the movie's schoolhouse is pictured here. Photo by Patty Salkeld

RIGHT: Situated outside of Vallejo in Solano County, Marineworld/Africa USA is home to a diverse array of wildlife. From compelling exhibits to breath-taking shows, this 160-acre park has something for every visitor. Photo by Gerald L. French/The Photo File

BELOW: Hot-air ballooning over lush Napa Valley vineyards makes for a memorable trip to California's world-famous wine country. Photo by Lee Foster/The Photo File

an alfresco champagne brunch. The sight of endless acres of carefully tended vineyards seen from above is one of the most memorable souvenirs of the California wine country.

The town of Calistoga perches at the north tip of the Napa Valley a bit of western Americana in a world of its own. Long famous for its natural mineral waters, Calistoga is home to a number of spas specializing in mineral and mud baths and massage treatments.

Solano County, east of Napa, is quickly gaining recognition as a tourist destination for two major reasons. One is Marine World/Africa USA, a 160-

main street lined with preserved buildings, antique shops, restaurants, and a renovated nineteenth-century hotel. The old port city has preserved the former capitol, an impressive brick building that is a must-see on the city's printed walking tour.

Situated across the Carquinez Strait from Benicia, Port Costa in Contra Costa County is a sleepy village offering a look at old California. One of the better views is from the scenic drive from Port Costa to Crockett, a cliff-hugger that offers excitement to drivers and cyclists.

Another glimpse into the past is provided at the nearby John Muir National Historic Site in

acre park encompassing attractions for the entire family. Located on the outskirts of Vallejo only blocks from Interstate 80, this popular site is home to an impressive array of wildlife, from Bengal tigers to killer whales to a fascinating exhibit devoted entirely to butterflies. Marine World/Africa USA is known for its innovative programs, including special demonstrations and many opportunities for children to get close to the smaller, gentler animals who live there.

Not far away the former state capital of Benicia retains much of its historic integrity with a long

Martinez. Muir, the revered naturalist whose name is still inextricably linked with Yosemite and the Sierra, lived here for some 24 years until his death in 1914. Many of his manuscripts have been preserved in this stately, 17-room Victorian mansion, now open to the public. The house is only a small part of the original 2,600-acre ranch.

To the west lies Mount Diablo State Park. There are 50 campsites with this 18,000-acre park, where the views are unsurpassed for 150 miles in all directions. Located in Danville, the 3,849-foot Mount Diablo can be seen from all over the Bay Area.

The Bay Area's many beaches and parks have volleyball courts that are often occupied by both serious spikers and casual enthusiasts. Photo by Bob Rowan/Progressive Image

Contra Costa County's shoreline is a long and variegated one. Besides offering water sports, its bayfront parks, such as Point Isabel Regional Shoreline, are a haven for joggers, bicyclists, dog walkers and the occasional fisherman.

At the University of California at Berkeley in Alameda County students are quick to discover the myriad parks and hiking trails that snake through the hills above the university town. The least developed is probably Wildcat Canyon Regional Park, once home to squatters and speculators and now part of the East Bay Municipal Utilities District (EBMUD). There is also a bicycle path along Nimitz Way from Inspiration Point, but there is more to see on foot in this park filled with grassy hillsides and wooded canyons and forestland.

The granddaddy of the East Bay park system is Charles Lee Tilden Regional Park, which locals refer to simply as Tilden. Highly developed, it is popular throughout the year for its miles of scenic

trails through diverse terrain.

Oakland's Lake Merritt provides an urban oasis in the form of a 155-acre body of water whose three-mile perimeter is flanked with parks, paths, and attractions. Located within walking distance of a revitalized downtown core, the lake is home to the Natural Science Center and Waterfowl Refuge, the latter of which attracts hundreds of migrating birds in the winter.

Children's Fairyland, a large but low-key amusement park, is also situated on the north shore of the lake. Children of all ages flock here in good weather to ride the merry-go-rounds, wander through an outdoor nursery-rhyme setting and enjoy regular performances of puppet theater. Adjacent is the Lakeside Park Garden Center, where native flowers and plants and a Japanese garden provide a serene setting in the middle of the East Bay's largest city.

It is possible to venture out onto the lake itself in a canoe or a sailboat available from the Sailboat

House. Other recreational activities here include jogging, bicycling and lawn bowling on carefully tended grounds.

For more rugged adventures, the East Bay Regional Park District features more than 40 parks spread among some 60,000 acres. Among the more popular destinations is Redwood Regional Park, which has several access points. Refurbished in 1982, Redwood Regional Park is particularly stunning during the fall, when old orchard trees and native maple and hazels change colors, providing a vivid contrast to the steady green of oak and redwood trees.

Situated on 525 acres off I-580 in the Oakland hills, the Knowland Park Oakland Zoo boasts more than 330 animals from all over the globe. There are two elephant shows every afternoon (except when the zoo is closed between Thanksgiving and Christmas) and a petting zoo that children adore. Besides the animals, attractions include picnic and barbecue facilities and rides on an old-fashioned carousel and a miniature train.

West of Alameda County lies the county of San Mateo, which boasts the most accessible stretch of coastline in Northern California. Ideal for tidepooling, when the rocky portions of the shore reveal their hidden treasures of hermit crabs and sea anemones, the San Mateo coast offers much more in the way of outdoor recreation.

San Mateo County's best-known oceanfront town is Half Moon Bay, a still-quaint enclave of quiet streets, a few stores and a couple of bed-and-breakfast inns. Nearby are golf courses and horse stables that rent mounts for galloping along the water's edge.

On the north tip of this crescent-shaped bay, the village of Princeton-by-the-Sea is a well-known fishing port. In addition to hosting a professional fishing industry, Princeton's harbor is also home to a number of charter vessels. These can be rented

Miles of hiking and backpacking trails crisscross the hilly area of 67,000-acre Henry Coe State Park near the town of Gilroy. Black oak and big-leaf maple highlight the area. Photo by Bob Rowan/Progressive Image

for group fishing expeditions in search of salmon or other denizens of the deep. During the winter and spring months from late December until early April, the harbor is also the setting-off point for thrilling whale-watching cruises. This is the migrating season of the California gray whales, which travel between the rich feeding waters of Alaska to the warm breeding waters of Baja California. It is not uncommon to sight one of these awesome mammals breaching (leaping entirely out of the ocean) as close as one-half mile to shore. There are, of course, no guarantees, but one's odds of seeing one of these creatures is much better on the high seas than from the shore.

Perhaps the best beach for tidepooling is the James V. Fitzgerald Marine Reserve, a little north of Half Moon Bay. Picnic areas and hiking trails, nearby restaurants and grocery stores, and a family atmosphere make this sandy park a popular destination.

Montara State Beach is a half-mile-long swath of sand ideal for horseback riding, though it is also popular for volleyball and playing Frisbee.

South of Half Moon Bay, San Gregorio State Beach boasts white sand, a portion of which is usually devoted to nude sunbathing. High bluffs provide privacy and a windbreak.

In southern San Mateo, Ao Nuevo State Reserve is admittedly one of California's most spectacular natural areas. Sand dunes dot a penin-

sula; tidepools and nature trails beckon to explorers; and wildlife is abundant. Between December and March reservations are necessary to observe the enormous elephant seals that congregate here during the birthing season. The park is open to the public the rest of the year and is especially lovely during the spring wildflower season.

Northern California's premiere amusement park is Great America, which offers the latest in dizzying rides along with old-fashioned entertainment such as the carousel and hand-carved horses created for the park's opening in 1976. Names such as Revolution and Sky Whirl hint at the vertigo to come, while other, less jaw-dropping attractions include musical performances and greetings by creatures such as Yogi Bear and the Smurfs. Five simulated towns evoke America's past: a New England fishing village, a rural town from the 1920s, a part of the Alaskan frontier, a county fair and livestock exhibition, and a glimpse into the antebellum Deep South at Orleans Place.

South of San Jose is the 67,000-acre Henry W. Coe State Park. Miles of hiking and backpacking trails crisscross the hilly area near the town of Gilroy. Terrain ranges from open grassland to glens of black oak and big-leaf maple, which are particularly enchanting in the autumn. Of special interest is a botanical "island" consisting of ponderosa pine, a tree more common in the Sierra Nevada.

▲ SPECTATOR SPORTS

Bay Area residents are famous for their devotion to fitness, health and sports, and even those who don't participate in sports are usually avid fans of one of the region's several professional sports teams. From football to baseball to basketball to horse racing, some kind of sporting event can be found in the area virtually year round.

The hordes of fans who have seen the San Francisco '49er football team through thick and thin are called the " '49er Faithful." Old-timers may recall the thin times, but anyone who moved to the Bay Area in the past six years simply wouldn't believe this championship team ever lost a season.

As for baseball, the San Francisco Giants will finish this season at Candlestick Park. At the time of this printing however, it appears likely that the Giants will be moving next year to a new home in San Jose, Sacramento or St. Petersburg, Florida.

Of course the East Bay has its own team—the

San Francisco Giant Will Clark, a local favorite, always receives a hearty welcome from Bay Area sports fans. Photo by Chromosohm/ Sohm

Oakland Athletics—who met the Giants in the historic Bay-ball World Series of 1989. (Most people, of course, recall the game scheduled for October 17 of that year since it was upstaged by the Loma Prieta earthquake.)

The Athletics (or the Oakland A's as they are known) play their home games at the Oakland Coliseum, which enjoys delightful weather and fabulous boxes as well as standard seating. The premium seats may sell out in advance, but weekdays it is usually easy to pick up a ticket at the gate on the day of the game.

The Golden State Warriors play other professional basketball teams at the Oakland Coliseum Arena, next door to the open-air Coliseum.

One of the oldest tennis competitions, now known as the Volvo Men's Tennis Championships, was once held at the Cow Palace (where it was known as the Transamerica). Now this annual event is the first on the schedule of the American Tennis Circuit and is played in February on

indoor courts at the Civic Auditorium in central San Francisco.

The Bay Area is best known for sophisticated indoor entertainment, but it is also home to classic Wild West events from livestock shows to rodeos. The most famous of these is the Grand National Rodeo and Livestock Show, usually held in October at the enormous Cow Palace, located south of San Francisco in Daly City. In the summer, usually in August, the Cow Palace hosts the annual San Francisco Equestrian Festival, which features competitions in dressage and vaulting as well as in other categories.

The Greater Bay Area's temperate climate accommodates year-round thoroughbred horse racing. From January until June races begin at 12 noon Wednesday through Sunday at Golden Gate Fields, the bayside track off Interstate 80 in Albany. As soon as the season ends in the East Bay, it begins again in the South Bay at Bay Meadows in San Mateo, where post time is 1 p.m. the rest of the year.

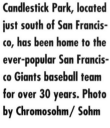

Candlestick Park, located just south of San Francisco, has been home to the ever-popular San Francisco Giants baseball team for over 30 years. Photo by Chromosohm/ Sohm

Northern California sunsets are as spectacular as any in the state. Ocean Beach lies west of Golden Gate Park and although heavy riptides discourage swimming, most San Franciscans like to walk on the cool sand and watch the bold colors of a Pacific Ocean sunset.
Photo by Kerrick James

CULTURAL COLLAGE

by Marty Olmstead

arly each September the sidewalks leading to San Francisco's beaux arts-style War Memorial Opera House overflow with onlookers and press photographers as lucky ticket holders sweep past on their way to the gala heralding the opening of the city's annual performing arts season.

A similar scene is enacted the same week as the San Francisco Symphony tunes up across the street beyond the

One of the most well-known Bay Area ethnic festivals is the Chinese New Year's celebration in San Francisco, which features a number of festivities leading up to the grand parade. This parade ends up in Chinatown and is followed by an awe-inspiring display of fireworks. Photo by Kerrick James

❑ ❑ ❑

glass facade of the eight-year-old Davies Symphony Hall. Throughout the fall less prestigious but equally anticipated openings characterize the height of the season. By Thanksgiving the San Francisco Ballet troupe will begin pirouetting across the Opera House stage and begin its program with its legendary productions of the "Nutcracker Suite."

These high-priced ticket events are only a glimmer, however, of the Bay Area's smorgasbord of cultural offerings. Touring musicals grace the planks of other performing arts houses. Some 40 small theater groups in San Francisco alone mount more modest (but often more avant-garde) productions. Symphony orchestras, jazz combos and chamber groups play throughout the year in San Jose, Oakland, Marin County and elsewhere.

From its offerings of Rachmaninoff to rock and Shakespeare to Tom Stoppard, the Bay Area is blessed with a bounty of cultural diversions. And there's more, including museums devoted to everything from traditional European paintings to rare Oriental jades to collections of Egyptian, Jewish, Mexican, Italian and Chinese treasures.

Ethnic diversity has characterized the Bay Area from the beginning. San Francisco has been called the most European-style American city and the most Asian of occidental communities. From the Dutch windmills on Golden Gate Park's sandy dunes to the dragon-shaped lampposts of Chinatown, the international influence is evident everywhere in San Francisco.

Throughout the city and its environs, it's easy to trace the waves of immigrants: Italian, Chinese, Irish, German, English and Japanese; then

Filipino, Vietnamese, Laotian, Taiwanese and even Samoan and Tongan. Cappuccino, bocce ball, Thai barbecue, high tea, shiatsu, sushi, shark's fin soup, dim sum and paté de foie gras are not considered exotica here but, rather, are familiar items in a cross-cultural kaleidoscope. Oakland boasts street signs in Chinese calligraphy. San Mateo County is headquarters for an ever-growing Filipino community. In San Francisco it is possible to experience several nationalities in the course of a day. You can spend the night in a fine French hotel, shop for Scottish woolens and Italian luggage all morning, view Asian art in the afternoon and see Russian opera at night.

San Francisco spearheaded the cultural evolution of the entire West Coast. As a nineteenth-century writer observed, San Francisco is a city that was never a town. Over the decades it has become internationally recognized as a center for fine arts. Its opera company is considered one of the best in the world; its symphony is now housed in a $27-million hall; its ballet performances are so good that they are televised and its leading repertory group is the country's largest.

Inevitably, the same yearnings for sophisticated entertainment spilled over the city's boundaries. Berkeley, Oakland, San Jose and Marin County all boast thriving fine arts companies and museums. Whatever musical, opera, ballet, drama or comedy is not produced locally will, sooner or later, tour the Bay Area at one locale or another.

The consistent support of corporations, city funds and enthusiastic patrons has ensured the survival of one of the richest cultural environments in the country.

▲ THE SAN FRANCISCO OPERA

It's true in many ways that the place seemed to sprout overnight, offering entertainments that were rare in pioneer days. Even the forty-niners, fresh from the gold diggings, were treated to operatic performances more than a century ago.

In the very early days, men were often called upon to play women's roles. Today acclaimed singers such as Placido Domingo and Luciano Pavarotti grace the stage at the elegant War Memorial Opera House. Built in 1932, just nine years after the San Francisco Opera Company was founded, the opera house remains the centerpiece of the city's cultural scene. The opera company has presented countless American premieres and counts among its stateside debuts such names as Ranata Tebaldi, Birgit Nilsson and designer-director Jean-Pierre Ponnelle. The 10-opera, 70-performance season always includes masterpieces and surprises. The San Francisco Opera was one of the first to utilize supertitles (English translations projected above the stage) for operas sung in other languages.

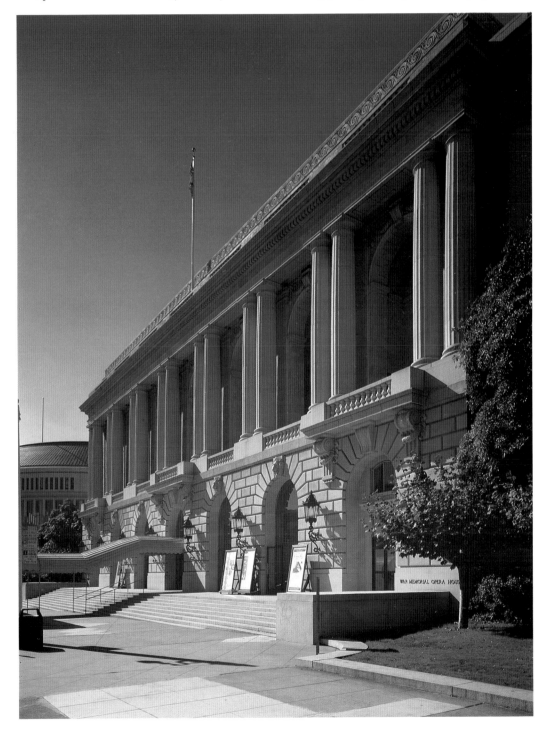

Home to the San Francisco Opera Company, the stately War Memorial Opera House was constructed in 1932 and is still the centerpiece of the city's cultural community. Photo by Gerald L. French/The Photo File

▲ POCKET OPERA

Not all of the city's operatic thrills are limited to black-tie evenings at the opera house. Among the city's most charming entertainments are the bare-bones versions of major operas mounted by Donald Pippin's Pocket Opera. The comic operas are particularly engaging, often hilarious. All operas are sung by local performers in English, and the costumes and sets are minimal. The libretto is also scaled down, making these a fabulous choice for novice opera lovers as well as aficionados who know the scores by heart.

▲ THE SYMPHONY

The regular season of the San Francisco Symphony Orchestra is headquartered in the Davies Symphony Hall, whose construction in 1980 made the Civic Center the largest performing arts complex in the country outside of New York City. None of this would have been possible without the paramount generosity of Louise Davies, whose donation to the city's cultural life is recognized far and wide. Founded in 1909, the symphony enjoys solid, widespread patronage both within and outside of the city. Programs, which often include

The San Francisco Symphony was founded in 1909 and today is considered one of the best in the world. The symphony enjoys solid, widespread patronage both inside and outside the city. Photo by Mark E. Gibson

some new music, are frequently presented in Berkeley and San Jose. In addition to the regular season between early September and May, the symphony typically presents a Beethoven Festival in June and a Summer Pops series in August.

Many Bay Area residents are unaware that the San Jose Symphony is even older than San Francisco's. With the exception of 1944-1946, the San Jose Symphony season has been running continuously since 1880. Modern seasons, which last from September through May, consist of three different series: Masterworks, Super Pops, and Favorite Classics.

And the new kid on the block is the Oakland East Bay Symphony, which presented its first concert in 1989. It currently performs from February through June.

Philharmonia Baroque Variety is the hallmark of the city's musical landscape. For the music of seventeenth and eighteenth-century composers, the Philharmonia Baroque presents works by Handel, Vivaldi, and Mozart throughout the winter, usually performing in the intimate Herbst Theatre in the Civic Center.

▲ LIVE THEATER

The heartbeat of Bay Area drama is the theater district located slightly west of Union Square along Geary Street. Over the decades, however, the interest in live theater has continued to mushroom, inspiring producers to open new theaters or to rehabilitate older ones to accommodate an apparently insatiable appetite. As a result, the Bay Area is one of America's most vital centers for the performing arts, perhaps eclipsed only by Chicago and New York for quantity. From their staples of European repertoire to the cutting edge of American and Asian works and from their Broadway musicals to local productions, Bay Area communities offer everything one could want.

In addition to evening performances, Sunday matinees are common. Best of all, it is possible to obtain half-price tickets to many of the better theaters in town. The STBS ticket outlet on Union Square in San Francisco sells direct to the public on the day of the performance.

The reigning monarch of Bay Area stage has long been the American Conservatory Theater. Rebounding from recent personnel changes and other

Louise Davies' donation to the cultural life of the Bay Area is the $27-million symphony hall that bears her name. The construction of the hall in 1980 made San Francisco's Civic Center the largest performing arts complex in the country outside of New York City. Photo by Amy Seidman-Tighe

troubles, ACT has regained its firm grasp of leadership and offers a highly diversified series of works each season. Since 1975 the group has opened for the Christmas season with Dickens' well-known take of Ebenezer Scrooge, *A Christmas Carol*. Any given season is likely to run the gamut from Shakespeare to Tom Stoppard to Woody Allen to Tennessee Williams, and now ACT has expanded around the corner to the New Stage Door Theater on Mason Street.

For all the theater offerings vying for their attention and time, San Franciscans still have time to pay homage to certain cult classics. A perennial favorite is the self-renewing musical series *Beach*

Musicians outside of U.C. Berkeley entertain students and passersby with acoustic renditions of familiar tunes. Photo by Mark E. Gibson

Blanket Babylon at Club Fugazi in North Beach.

The south side of San Francisco offers even more theaters, including the Julian Theatre on Potrero Hill, the Eureka Theatre in the Mission and the Asian American Theatre in the middle of town.

All the Bay Area seems to be a stage. The San Jose Repertory Company plays not only on the peninsula, but visits the city as well, playing at places such as the Montgomery Theatre. There are two theaters in Fort Mason, San Francisco's waterfront cultural compound. Up north the Marin Theatre Company can be found in Mill Valley and in Berkeley the Black Repertory Group specializes

in premiering works by the country's most exciting black playwrights. Also in the East Bay the acclaimed Berkeley Repertory Theatre offers an ambitious season virtually every year, taking on such plays as Shaw's *Man and Superman* with deft professionalism.

Summertime finds actors and props moving outdoors along with picnic baskets and ice coolers. The most famous playwright of all time, William Shakespeare, gets his due in the Bay Area with several summer festivals devoted entirely to the Bard's works. Some of Shakespeare's most beloved plays, such as *Midsummer Night's Dream* and *The Taming of the Shrew*, are particularly adaptable to outdoor performances. There are summertime Shakespeare festivals each year in Berkeley, San Francisco and Santa Cruz.

Cabarets and small revues can be found in just about every Bay Area town large enough for a freeway exit. It is impressive to see how many small cities now boast their own performance companies and theaters.

Concord, which only a decade ago was considered an outpost of civilization, is now the envy of bigger cities. The Concord Pavilion arena, a circular stage open on three sides to a sloping lawn, is an exciting venue for music and other entertainments from spring through the fall. It also stands as testimony that public service and successful business operations can coexist with benefits for everyone.

Tucked in a valley within view of soaring Mount Diablo, the Concord Pavilion seats 3,769 people under its one-acre roof and another 5,000 on the thickly turfed lawns encircling the seats. A highly adaptable stage has been graced by rock bands such as Dire Straits, chanteuses such as Liza Minnelli, and all manner of jazz, rhythm and blues, symphonic and other types of music.

On the peninsula the Shoreline Amphitheater sports giant video screens so fans can get even better views of their favorite rock stars at this popular facility in Mountain View.

The stage at Great America, the Santa Clara amusement park, is also in demand during summer evenings for performances by singers and musicians.

The enviable Bay Area weather also bestows its blessings on Mount Tamalpais, which has its own natural amphitheater at 2,000 feet above sea level.

The views are spectacular, even when there are no performances at the 5,000-seat Mountain Theater. This area is part of a generous parcel donated in 1915 by William Kent, a member of a prominent local family still residing in Marin County. In the 1930s the Civilian Conservation Corps fashioned some rows of seats out of serpentine that had been carried down from the west peak. Even before that

visitors had long flocked to enjoy the annual Mountain Play, which is held in the spring, as well as other dramatic productions, concerts, weddings and religious services.

A member of another Bay Area family also left his stamp on the Bay Area outdoor theater community. The 175-acre estate, park, and cultural center known as Villa Montalvo was one of the last great estates built in California before World War I. James Duval Phelan, formerly a three-term mayor of San Francisco, established the grounds and an Italian Renaissance villa in the countryside near Saratoga. Constructed in time to debut at the 1915 Panama-Pacific Exposition, Villa Montalvo reflects the classic serenity of Spain and Italy. Although he followed in the steps of his banker/merchant father, Phelan never forsook his first love: the literary and artistic life of the Bay Area. Upon his death in 1930, Phelan bequeathed part of his estate to the continuation of the villa as a place where artists, writers and performers could carry on their cultural endeavors. And it is still going strong.

LEFT: Summer months in the Bay Area inspire many outdoor theater productions. Even San Francisco's famed cable cars can become the backdrop for innovative productions. Photo by Gerald L. French/The Photo File

BELOW: The Concord Pavilion seats 3,769 people under its one-acre roof and another 5,000 on the thickly turfed lawns encircling the seats. Situated in a valley within view of Mount Diablo, the pavilion contains a circular stage that opens on three sides to a sloping lawn. Photo by Bob Rowan/ Progressive Image

FACING PAGE: The town of Novato in Marin County is host to the annual Renaissance Pleasure Faire, which is held every autumn in September and October. Photo by Lee Foster/The Photo File

▲ SAN FRANCISCO FILM FESTIVAL

Though filmmaking is usually equated with Southern California, the Bay Area boasts distinction in this medium as well as in more traditional fine arts. For example, the concept of film festivals, which originated in Italy, was first adopted in the United States by the San Francisco Film Festival more than 30 years ago. The format and dates have changed, but the festival still carries considerable cachet. It is one of the most popular events in the Bay Area, which is impressive considering its consistent inclusion of foreign-made films. One of the early directors of the festival, Albert Johnson, pioneered the idea of formal tributes to stars as well as movie directors—an idea that has been widely accepted all over the world. Luminaries such as Edward G. Robinson, John Ford, Fred Astaire, Bernardo Bertolucci, Bette Davis and Paul Newman have all received their due in retrospectives at the San Francisco Film Festival. Tickets to the opening-night festivities are among the most sought-after in town.

▲ PACIFIC FILM ARCHIVE

Across the bay another institution receives considerable acclaim of its own. Housed in the University Art Museum on the University of California campus at Berkeley, the Pacific Film Archive is an invaluable resource for scholars, students and everyday movie buffs. It contains research materials and facilities and several screening rooms where it is possible to see some of the archive's extensive collection of films dating from the beginning of the movie industry. A great plus, particularly for those

who live in the East Bay, is the archive's enviable schedule—two different films are shown nightly.

▲ FESTIVALS

Overall, one of the best and most delightful introductions to the kaleidoscope of Bay Area culture is attendance at one of the numerous festivals held throughout the year.

Perhaps the Bay Area's most well-known festival is the Chinese New Year's celebration, which features a number of festivities leading up to the grand parade, always accompanied by fireworks, in the heart of San Francisco's Chinatown.

Late April brings the Cherry Blossom Festival. Always held on two consecutive weekends in spring, the Cherry Blossom Festival has blossomed into an international event, attracting dancers and musicians from the Far East as well as from the United States. Martial arts demonstrations, exhibits of ikebana (flower arranging) and origami (paper works), beauty pageants, food booths and general merriment precede the final Sunday, when an enormous colorful parade snakes through the city to its destination in the heart of Nihonmachi, San Francisco's own Japantown.

Every spring San Francisco celebrates Carnival with endless Latin music, dancing, and a massive parade that winds its way through the heavily Latino Mission District.

Then there is Columbus Day, when all of North Beach becomes Italian, and St. Patrick's Day, when the entire Bay Area is Irish for a day. (Local chambers of commerce and visitors and convention bureaus are the best sources for festival calendars.)

The Pacific Film Archive, located on the University of California campus at Berkeley, contains research materials and facilities where it is possible to view some of the archive's extensive collection of films dating from the beginning of the motion picture industry. Photo by Amy Seidman-Tighe

ABOVE: San Francisco's Castro district is the place to be on Halloween night. Photo by Rory Lysaght/ The Photo File

RIGHT: The Cinco de Mayo parade winds through the streets of San Francisco. Photo by Kerrick James

▲ MUSEUMS

Living in the Bay Area is often like a long vacation in a favorite foreign city. Bay Area museumgoers can pet starfish, see ancient mummies, get a tattoo, look at photographs of the Gold Rush days, test their visual perception, watch cable cars operate, walk the decks of old sailing vessels or sign up for a culinary tour of Chinatown. The number of museums and the varieties of delights they hold is one of the region's crowning glories. Of course there are more traditional collections, particularly in European paintings and Orientalia, but it's the mix that makes the excitement. Spending an afternoon in a museum is not something Northern Californians do only when they go away on vacation; it's as popular a local pastime as skating in Golden Gate Park or sampling espresso in North Beach.

Within 1,000-acre Golden Gate Park in San Francisco are some of the best museums on the West Coast, including the M.H. de Young Memorial Museum, the Asian Art Museum and the California Academy of Sciences.

The M.H. de Young Memorial Museum is the most diversified museum, with permanent collections detailing western civilization from its beginnings in ancient Greece, Rome and Egypt through the tumult of the Middle Ages and the glories of the Renaissance up to the present. More than 40 galleries display humankind's most civilized graphic achievements, from pre-Columbian artifacts to twentieth-century paintings by famous European and American artists. Enthusiastically supported by a membership base and enhanced by visitors from all over the Bay Area and beyond, the de Young also hosts traveling exhibits such as the monumental King Tut show and one of Tiffany glassworks.

Next door the Asian Art Museum stands as testimony to the Bay Area's rewarding relationship with its cultural cousins across the Pacific. Constructed in 1966, when connoisseur Avery Brundage chose to bequeath his vast collection to the City of San Francisco, the Asian Art Museum is a trove of riches from China, India, Japan, Korea, Tibet and other Far East and Near East countries. The Chinese collection alone spans some 4,000 years and includes ancient pottery and antique bronzes and more. It requires repeat visits even to begin to see this museum's holdings, which are so extensive that only about 10 percent can be displayed at any given time. A perfect capper to a tour here is to enjoy tea and cookies at the adjacent Japanese Tea Garden, a secluded spot that exudes Oriental peace and charm.

The museums in Golden Gate Park are arranged so compactly that it is possible to visit three in the course of a day. A refreshing change from the musty, high-brow collection across the way are the living exhibits displayed at the California Academy of Sciences. Founded in 1853, it is the oldest scientific institution on the entire West Coast. In fact, it is really three museums in one: the Steinhart Aquarium, a planetarium, and a natural history museum.

Other nature-oriented museums and other educational and cultural facilities in the Bay Area cater to families. In San Mateo County the multilevel Coyote Point Museum gives the best introduction to Bay Area ecology available anywhere. Nature stories, beachcombing, plant identification, birdwatching, slide and film shows and, best of all, hands-on exhibits easily fill an afternoon. Experienced visitors frequently allow time for a walk around the grounds and perhaps a picnic within view of the southern portion of San Francisco Bay.

Another fun-but-educational museum is the Musee Mechanique in San Francisco's renowned Cliff House, where music boxes and coin-operated mechanical games hark back to the years when Playland-at-the-Beach attracted crowds to its amusement park delights only a few yards south of the restaurant.

Some of the Bay Area's finest museums are located on the campuses of its colleges and universities. The De Saisset Museum, for instance, is located at California's oldest institution of higher learning, Santa Clara University, which was built in 1851 on the grounds of the Mission Santa Clara de Asis. Established through a bequest of Isabel de Saisset on behalf of her brother, painter Ernest de Saisset, the museum has expanded its art collection to include paintings, prints and sculpture by both American and European artists from the sixteenth century to the present. In addition, the museum is distinguished by its collections of European and Asian decorative art and African tribal art. Changing exhibits, lectures, concerts, film series and other cultural offerings make the de Saisset an extremely valuable asset to life on the peninsula.

Some 30,000 Santa Clara Valley residents and tourists visit the university's California History

ABOVE AND FACING PAGE: The Palace of Fine Arts opened to the public in 1915 as part of the Panama-Pacific International Exposition. Its opening symbolized San Francisco's recovery from the devastating 1906 earthquake. Photos by Kerrick James

BELOW: The de Saisset Museum at Santa Clara University features works by both American and European artists from the sixteenth century to the present. Photo by Amy Seidman-Tighe

Collection galleries annually. These galleries have been expanded, reinterpreted, and reinstalled to reflect three historical periods: Indian, mission, and early college. The museum also has plans to further expand the section on the Costonoan Indians, focusing on their use of the land long before the missionaries arrived.

The intellectual life of the East Bay is centered at the University of California at Berkeley, which boasts a number of museums and galleries. The University Art Museum is one of the largest university art museums in the world. Designed by Mario J. Campi and opened in 1970, the museum is a spacious concrete building consisting of a series of terraces that lead from the terrace, where student works are displayed, up to the galleries that offer changing exhibitions.

Berkeley is endowed with the largest anthropological collection west of the Mississippi. More

ABOVE: Art lovers can choose from a variety of artistic and cultural opportunities in the Bay Area region. Pictured here is a Point Reyes gallery. Photo by Chris Springmann/The Photo File

RIGHT: The Museum of Modern Art (MOMA) in downtown San Francisco houses sculpture, paintings and photography by such notables as Diego Rivera and Georgia O'Keeffe. MOMA also contains a rental and retail gallery. Photo by Amy Seidman-Tighe

than half a million specimens are displayed at the Lowie Museum of Anthropology, only a smattering of the museum's vast holdings of archaeological material from Egypt, the Mediterranean, Peru and North America. The Lowie's collection of contemporary ethnographic material has been gathered from all over California as well as from the Pacific Islands, Asia and Africa. A marvelous

gift shop stocks unusual books as well as moderately priced folk art.

High in the scenic Berkeley hills is a very unusual museum, the Lawrence Hall of Science. This museum features engaging exhibits such as earthquake simulations and interactive experiments such as those in the Wizard's Lab. A planetarium, computer terminals, science-film programs and moving life-size dinosaur models keep visitors busy for visit after visit. Outside is a full-scale model of the space shuttle *Challenger's* cabin, a poignant reminder of those killed in America's tragic space program disaster. Perhaps most symbolic of this unique university town, however, is the nearby piece by Richard O'Hanlon, a creation of three granite stones aligns with the equinox, the North Star, moon and other celestial phenomena, an inspired collaboration between science and art.

Everywhere in the Bay Area residents are close to fascinating exhibits and museums of which many are devoted to interpreting the area's history. When it comes to California art, perhaps the best museum in the state is Oakland's Museum of California. Housed in an award-winning building in a parklike setting, this is a combination of exhibits and environments. The 1930s Gallery features paintings of that era by famous artists such as Maynard Dixon and John Langly Howard as well as later works such as the figurative paintings of Nathan Oliveira. Also on display are numerous significant pieces from the Arts and Crafts

movement in the state, from the late nineteenth century to the present. Known as a regional institution, the Museum of California also displays small-scale photography by Western legends such as Imogen Cunningham and Edward Weston.

Newcomers eager to get a feeling for California as a state have only to visit the Assay Office here, where the first Comstock Lode silver was assayed in 1860. Nearby are a pioneer family's kitchen and offbeat memorabilia such as Country Joe MacDonald's guitar. One of the most enduring exhibits is the Hall of California History, which is arranged as a time-capsule journey from prehistoric to modern times. The Oakland Museum is fine evidence of the possibilities inherent in taking a vertical, rather than a horizontal, approach to history. By focusing entirely on California, the museum offers an in-depth experience that is impossible in museums with a broader scope.

The banking industry, which played so large a role in the Bay Area's early development, has made large investments in maintaining links to the region's past. Wells Fargo, the bank most closely linked with California's Gold Rush days, has

captured its own 134-year history in a 1,000-item museum. The Wells Fargo History Museum, located in San Francisco's financial district, houses artifacts from the Old West such as original photographs, lithographs, etchings and documents that delineate the company's evolution from stagecoach days to automatic teller machine technology. The 4,400-square-foot museum is, appropriately, located on Montgomery Street, where the first Wells Fargo office opened in 1852.

In 1973 a museum devoted to the history of California's earliest residents opened in Marin County in a two-story house donated by Crocker Bank. The Miwok Museum in Novato contains artifacts found in a nearby archaeological site, along with artwork from tribes from Alaska all the way to South America. Particularly educational is a display showing the ways Indians used tule, a low bulrush marsh plant easily found around the Bay Area. The Miwoks wove tule into receptacles for food, for moccasins and leggings, and even for building houses and canoes. Also in Miwok Park is a coastal Indian village archaeological site and a garden of native California plants that played a

Learning Wall, **by Keith Sklar, is one of the many murals that can be found throughout San Francisco. Walking mural tours are available for those who want to learn more about the city's muralist tradition. Photo by Chromosohm/Sohm**

central role in Miwok life long before the Spaniards arrived.

Farther north two museums in Napa County draw visitors who want to know more about the history of the famous wine-growing region. The Sharpsteen Museum and Sam Brannan Cottage, located in downtown Calistoga, were donated to the City in 1976 by Ben Sharpsteen, who retired here after 30 years with Walt Disney Studios. Aside from exhibits from Sharpsteen's career and on such exotica as the evolution of the California license plate, the museum is best known for its dioramas recreating the arrival of the railroad and life in the local Chinatown. Dedicated to Calistoga's earliest settlers, the Sharpsteen Museum houses replicas of a pioneer California kitchen and an old-fashioned blacksmith's shop. The Brannan cottage, furnished with period furniture, including an antique piano, offers its own glimpse into the past. Most enchanting is the miniature recreation of the health resort as it looked in 1865. (The town got its name, the story goes, when Sam Brannan made a speech in which he meant to compare his resort town with its counterpart in New York, a place called Saratoga. In a slip of the tongue, he called it "the Calistoga of

Sarafornia," and thus the place was christened.)

Down the highway in St. Helena the unofficial capital of the wine country, the Silverado Museum opened in 1969 to commemorate the 75th anniversary of the death of Robert Louis Stevenson. Like hundreds of writers since that time, Stevenson was drawn to Napa, where he spent part of his 1880 honeymoon in an abandoned bunkhouse on nearby Mount St. Helena. The experience is chronicled in his book, *The Silverado Squatters*. This museum amassed more than 8,000 items acquired from friends and heirs of the author: letters and manuscripts, paintings and sculptures, photographs and other memorabilia.

The Bay Area's melting pot of cultures, philosophies and religions is evident in Berkeley's Judah L. Magnes Museum. Jewish life, history and religion from ancient times to the present day are preserved in art, artifacts, documents and photographs as well as in two libraries. The museum rotates exhibits on various Jewish themes and houses records of marriages, bar mitzvahs and other events in its library of West American Jewry. This Berkeley mansion, located in a residential neighborhood, also contains a bookshop.

The rebuilding of a steam locomotive can be witnessed at the Railroad Museum in Solano County's community of Rio Vista. Photo by Mark E. Gibson

San Francisco, too, has its share of ethnic-oriented museums, from the Chinese Cultural Museum in Chinatown to the Museo Italo-Americano and the Mexican Museum, the latter both located in an intriguing Marina District complex known as Fort Mason. Established as an army post in the eighteenth century, Fort Mason was expanded by WPA workers in the 1930s. Today it has become a nationally recognized pioneer in community arts circles. Few cities can boast so many cultural organizations clustered at a single address.

Now part of the vast Golden Gate National Recreation Area, Fort Point consists of several wharfside warehouses sheltering an impressive array of museums, theaters, galleries, workshops and restaurants. In addition, it is the site of annual fairs such as the Christmastime folk arts exhibit and sale. The Mexican Museum, originally established in the heart of the Latin settlement in the Mission, was relocated to Fort Point a few years ago. Here the Mexican heritage of many Californians is revealed through an enviable collection that ranges from pre-Columbian artifacts and colonial art to modern Chicano paintings and murals. As with most of the city's museums, there is an excellent gift shop adjoining the display areas.

Similarly, the Museo Italo-Americano was relocated from its natural home in North Beach to this

complex. Displays of historical and current Italian and Italian-American art and photographs change every other month.

The Bay Area's preeminence as a world leader in science and technology is also woven into the fabric of everyday life. A few blocks west of Fort Point is the Exploratorium, arguably the best science museum anywhere in the world. Its plethora of interactive exhibits allows visitors to push, pull, swing, toss, manipulate and/or focus on all manner of displays and objects, the better to understand various principles such as prisms, sound, electricity, laser, mathematics, animal and plant behavior, and, believe it or not, even more. Ongoing lectures, changing exhibits and a first-rate staff make this 20-year-old attraction a perennial favorite for Bay Area residents who love to play tourist in their own backyard.

The Exploratorium couldn't have a more fitting home than the equally impressive Palace of Fine Arts, which was built in 1915 in time for the Panama-Pacific Exposition.

The Rosicrucian Egyptian Museum claims to be San Jose's number-one tourist attraction, outdrawing even the famed Winchester Mystery House. This is the kind of site that appeals to visitors from all over the world and lures even sophisticated San Franciscans down the peninsula for a peek. The Rosicrucians, who call their association "The Ancient, Mystical Order Rosae Crucis," are a worldwide fraternal and educational order that has established a museum, planetarium and science museum in San Jose, their world headquarters. One of the most intriguing exhibits is a walk-in tomb modeled after ancient tombs dating from about 2000 B.C. The only recreation of its kind in the United States, it houses a replica of the sarcophagus of King Tutankhamen. The mummy, however, is only one highlight of this unique museum. It also contains the West Coast's largest collection of Egyptian, Babylonian and Assyrian artifacts, including alabaster jars and stone jewelry and countless other relics. Aside from the Near East collections, one of the more interesting exhibits concerns early discoveries in mathematics and linguistics.

FACING PAGE: The Rosicrucian Egyptian Museum is San Jose's number-one tourist attraction. A recreation of a walk-in tomb from about 2000 B.C. remains the most intriguing exhibit. The tomb houses a replica of the sarcophagus of King Tutankhamen—the only one of its kind in the United States. Photo by Amy Seidman-Tighe

BELOW: The Bay Area's environmental art brings together the properties of physics and the surrounding environment to create a unique vision in Contra Costa County's Lafayette Hills. Photo by Bob Rowan/Progressive Image

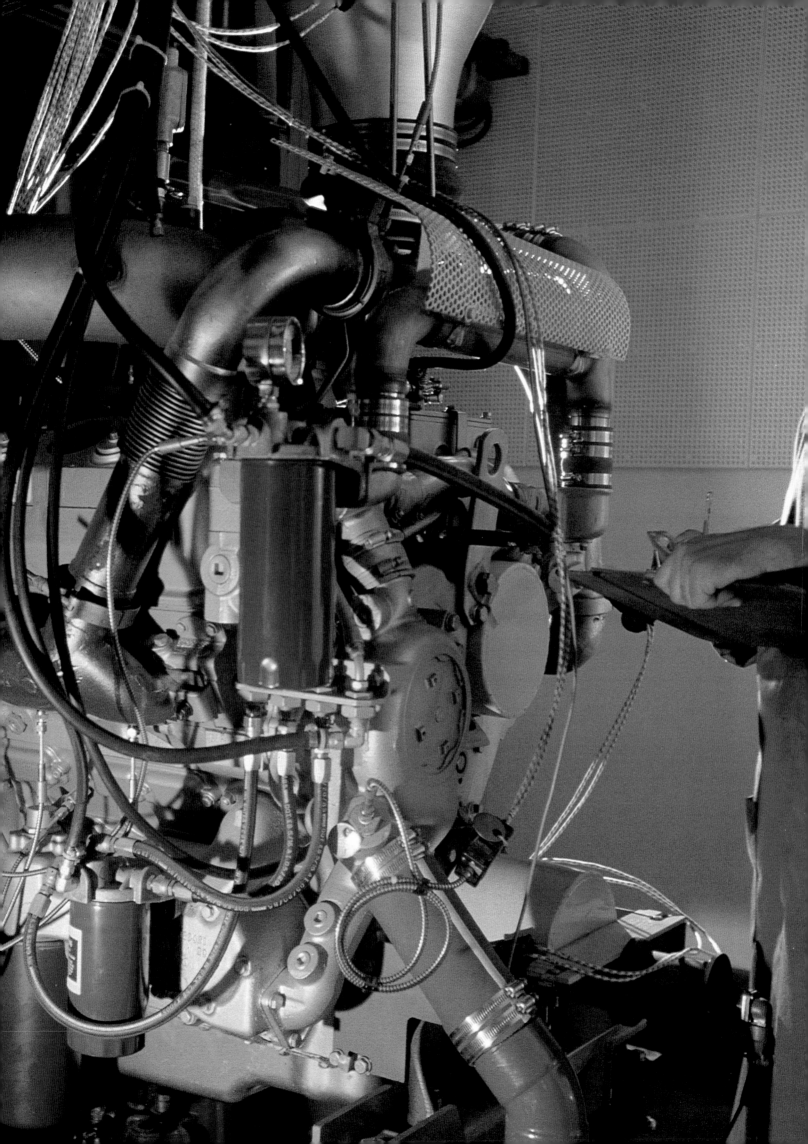

BIRTHPLACE OF IDEAS, DOORWAY TO THE FUTURE

by John K. Waters

The Bay Area has been described as "...the densest concentration of innovative industry that exists anywhere in the world." From computer chips to customized bacteria, from medical lasers to microscopic motors, the region's numerous high-technology companies have produced a torrent of products that have literally changed the world.

Jock Bockman examines data at the Chevron Research Laboratory in Richmond. Chevron has reduced, through research and technology, some 72 percent of the pollutants from its own industrial waste products and has removed 50 percent of the pollutants from its refineries' air emissions. Photo by Amy Seidman-Tighe

❑ ❑ ❑

The Bay Area is a leader in the challenging field of high technology. Photo by John Lund/The Photo File

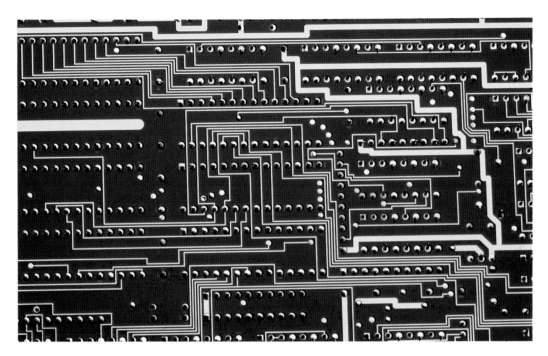

Many forces have shaped the remarkable evolution of the Bay Area's high-tech industries, but without a doubt, the single most important influence has been the pioneering research of scientists, engineers and scholars at work in local universities and hospitals. Cutting-edge technology companies often choose to locate their operations in the Bay Area specifically because of the region's proximity to first-class universities and teaching hospitals.

"This is where the real talent is," explains Satish Kumar, vice president of California Micro Devices' Magnetic Head Division in Milpitas. "There are more qualified, motivated people available to employers [in high-technology companies] in this area than any other place in the country."

According to Eve Majure, manager of university programs for the American Electronics Association, local electronics companies work closely with Bay Area universities, funding research and working to make curricula more industry-relevant.

"It's critical [for high tech companies] to locate near major research universities," she says. "They are the source of their engineering hires. This is somewhat less important to large companies who deal with research universities all over the country, but geographical proximity is especially important for the smaller electronics firms."

High-tech firms in the Bay Area are able to draw from a steady flow of top-flight graduates in science and engineering. Between them, Stanford University in Palo Alto and its illustrious neighbor across the bay, the University of California at Berkeley, have counted among their faculty a total of 21 Nobel Laureates—a national record. And, according to a survey by *Science Digest,* the Bay Area is home to at least one-third of the best American scientists under age 40.

Is it any wonder then that the Bay Area is known for having more Ph.D.'s per square mile than any other place on earth?

More than a mere magnet for high-tech companies, the Bay Area is the birthplace of high technology. Without the development of the transistor and the klystron tube by Stanford professors, Santa Clara County's world-famous Silicon Valley would be filled with fruit orchards instead of computer company campuses; without the ground-breaking medical research of scientists at Stanford Medical Center, UC Berkeley, and UC San Francisco, the East Bay's so-called "Biotech Alley" would simply not exist.

The Bay Area is home to some six public colleges and universities, 14 private colleges, five art/music schools/conservatories, 14 business/technical schools, five seminaries/bible colleges, one maritime academy, one alternative humanities college, one four-year school of fashion, and 22 community/ junior colleges. All serve the region with a variety of academic programs. When it comes to scientific research, however, three Bay Area institutions stand above the rest: Stanford, UC Berkeley and UC San Francisco.

Cutting-edge technology companies often choose to locate their operations in the Bay Area specifically because of the region's proximity to teaching hospitals and first-class universities. One such university, pictured here, is U.C. Berkeley. Photo by Gerald L. French/The Photo File

▲ Stanford University

Stanford University is one of the world's leading centers for new, high-technology development. The university has ranked consistently among the top five universities in federally sponsored research in fields ranging from engineering and particle physics to medical genetics.

Stanford was founded in 1885 by California Senator Leland Stanford and his wife, Jane, in memory of their only child, Leland, Jr., who died of typhoid fever the year before. The university is located immediately adjacent to Palo Alto on 8,200 acres of farmland formerly owned by the Stanfords (hence the nickname, "The Farm").

Stanford's founders were progressive for their time, establishing a nondenominational residential institution open to both sexes and affordable to all qualified students regardless of financial means. In fact, there was no tuition at Stanford until 1920, when a charge of $120 per year was instituted.

The university's present student population totals approximately 13,000 undergraduates and graduates and comprises top applicants from every state in the union as well as from many foreign countries.

Stanford's faculty, which totals 1,325, includes Nobel, Pulitzer and MacArthur Foundation Prize winners; National Medal of Science winners and members of the National Academies of Science, Engineering, Education, and Arts and Sciences. Since 1974 Stanford University faculty members have received more than 122 Guggenheim awards.

Stanford's ties to the development of Silicon Valley's electronics industries date as far back as 1909, when the university's first president, David Starr Jordan, encouraged a young graduate student named Cyrus Elwell to start a new business. Jordan went so far as to invest $500 in the firm, which later perfected the vacuum tube as a sound amplifier and a generator of electromagnetic waves, signally the birth of the electronics age.

The presence of a university with strong academic departments willing to work closely with local companies fueled the growth of the Santa Clara Valley's infant electronics industry, but the chief architect of that growth was the late Frederic Emmons Terman, a Stanford professor of electrical engineering who encouraged his students to start companies near campus. Among the students who followed Terman's advice were Bill Hewlett and David Packard. Two others were Dean Watkins and Dick Johnson.

Terman received a big assist from the Stanford physics department in 1937 when Professor William Hansen gave graduate student Russell Varian and his brother, Sigurd, work space and $100 for materials to develop the klystron tube. Their invention became the foundation of radar and microwave communications.

As university provost after World War II, Terman recognized the potential for combining federal research funds, academic programs, and industrial development. That combination led to the enhancement of academic departments at Stanford and to the creation of the Stanford Industrial Park (now called Stanford Research Park).

Stanford University is one of the world's leading centers for new high-technology development. The university has ranked consistently among the top five universities in federally sponsored research in fields ranging from engineering and particle physics to medical genetics. Photo by Mark E. Gibson

The Research Park's first tenant was Varian Associates, soon followed by the Hewlett-Packard and Watkins-Johnson companies.

Stanford's ties to the local electronics industry were considerably strengthened when, in 1955, William Shockley, co-inventor of the transistor, located his company, the Shockley Transistor Corporation, in the Research Park and joined the university's electrical engineering department as a member of the faculty.

Two years later, in one of the classic spin-offs of its kind, eight Shockley employees left to form Fairchild Semiconductor, where they co-invented the integrated circuit. Several engineers then spun off to form Intel Corporation, where the microprocessor was invented. The process continued to repeat itself; at last count, some 55 electronics firms have since evolved from Fairchild or its offspring.

The park continued to grow, attracting a Lockheed research laboratory that gave rise to the company's Missiles and Space Division in nearby Sunnyvale. Firms specializing in lasers, pharmaceuticals and biochemistry, and other fields followed, among them Syntex, IBM, Beckman Instruments and Xerox.

Today the 660-acre Stanford Research Park is home to some 55 high-tech firms employing some 25,000 people. Tenants are accepted only if their work ties in with the university's

St. Perpetua Elementary School in Contra Costa County makes computers a part of the classroom curriculum, giving its students a head start in computer literacy and education. Photo by Bob Rowan/Progressive Image

The Altamont Pass Windmills (as they are commonly known) generate electricity as part of ongoing research into alternative energy sources. Photo by Chromosohm/Sohm

research and instructional programs, thus cementing the ties between Stanford University and Silicon Valley that continues today.

The invention of the klystron tube provided the basic technology for, and led to the development of the first linear accelerator. The two-mile-long Stanford Linear Accelerator Center, which generates the highest energy electron beams available in the world, is located on 426 acres of Stanford University land and is a world center for high-energy physics research. For more than 20 years the Center has been in continuous use in a national research program that has made major contributions to human understanding of nature.

Operated by the U.S. Department of Energy, the Center is a single-purpose laboratory devoted to experimental and theoretical research in elementary particle physics and to the development of new techniques in high-energy accelerators and elementary particle detectors. For example: experiments with the linear accelerator have shown that the heart of the atomic nucleus, the proton, once thought to be the smallest particles of matter, is itself composed of still smaller particles, now called quarks.

Researchers working at the Stanford University Medical Center were the first in the Western Hemisphere to use a linear accelerator in the treatment of cancer. Known throughout the world for its outstanding research achievements, the Stanford Medical Center comprises the university's School of Medicine (the oldest medical school in the Western United States), the Stanford University Clinics, the Stanford University Hospital, and the Lucille Salter Packard Children's Hospital at Stanford, which opened in 1991.

The medical center's staff and faculty, which include some 580 teachers and 435 physicians, represent a singular combination of scientists in pursuit of basic research and clinicians closely involved in patient care. Close ties between the medical school and other schools and departments at Stanford University, such as physics, engineering, chemistry and computer science, have led to unique joint research programs. The Stanford Hospital and its staff also play a crucial role in many clinical studies.

Scientific research activities at Stanford University, the Stanford Linear Accelerator Center and the Stanford Medical Center are varied and far-reaching. Stanford researchers have been responsible for a number of important scientific contributions, which include, in small part:

• *the laser.* Arthur Schawlow's theoretical work at Stanford in laser spectroscopy led directly to the creation of the first laser by researchers at Howard Hughes Medical Institute. Schawlow won a Nobel Prize in 1981 for his contribution.

His research not only produced a device that has had an impact on a wide variety of markets in medicine (medical and dental lasers) and home entertainment (the compact disk), it also led to the creation of Spectra Physics, the largest laser company in the world. A host of other laser companies have since begun to exploit the commercial potential of laser technology.

In 1963 Stanford eye surgeons demonstrated the use of lasers to weld detached retinas in animals. This demonstration was followed by successful use of the treatment in human patients.

• *Nuclear Magnetic Resonance.* The discovery of nuclear magnetic resonance was made almost simultaneously by Felix Bloch at Stanford and E.M. Purcell at Harvard. The two scientists found that when atoms were dropped into a strong magnetic field, they would absorb certain radiowave frequencies and their cores would resonate or vibrate. Bloch and Purcell received the Nobel Prize in 1952, but most scientists at the time—including Bloch himself—did not realize the importance of this discovery.

Today physicians use magnetic resonance imaging (MRI) machines to diagnose heart disease and to detect brain tumors and other cancers accurately and non-invasively. Another application, magnetic resonance spectroscopy, is used to describe the fundamental properties of proteins and, in turn, the processes of life.

Stanford researchers in both medicine and engineering are currently working to refine MNR technology. An entirely new industry has emerged both in the U.S. and abroad to bring magnetic resonance imaging applications to the marketplace.

• *polymers.* In 1974 Paul J. Flory received the Nobel Prize in Chemistry for his work on polymers at Cornell and Stanford. Polymers, long molecules made by stringing atoms together in chemical reactions, are the basis for the plastics used in products ranging from coffeemakers and grinders to printers and computers.

• *human heart transplants.* In animal experiments that preceded the transplantation of the first human heart in South Africa by 10 years, Dr. Norman Shumway and Richard Lower at Stanford developed the surgical techniques as well as regimens to control rejection and had reported the first successful heart transplant in a dog.

By the time human heart transplantation had begun, Shumway's group had the experience and track record to enter the field with confidence, performing more than 600 heart transplants as of this writing. Shumway's group also succeeded in transplanting combined hearts and lungs and, more recently, has embarked on a new transplantation effort in children with incurable congenital heart and lung diseases.

One example of the practical application of agricultural research can be found in the wine cellar of Hess Vineyard. Its cellar was built into a mountainside to keep the wine cool in order to halt the fermentation process and allow the wine to age properly. Photo by Amy Seidman-Tighe

Apple Computer, Inc., a vanguard of the Silicon Valley's personal computer industry, has its corporate headquarters in Cupertino. Photo by Chromosohm/Sohm

• *the music synthesizer*: John Chowning developed computer chips that allowed a dramatic leap forward in the music synthesizer's ability to imitate other instruments. Every Yamaha DZ synthesizer contains these chips today.

• *artificial intelligence*: John McCarthy won the National Medal of Science for his contributions to the development of computer science. He coined the term "artificial intelligence" and originated time-sharing, which allows several people to use

the same computer at once. He has combined ideas from formal logic and made them effective on computers, leading to applications in industry, medicine and other fields.

• *healing skin*: A Stanford research group is one of only two in the nation working on techniques that allow a patient's own skin to be used as a sort of biological bandage. Especially important in healing burns, wounds, and non-healing ulcers, a small patch of the patient's skin can be taken by doctors

As a major city in Santa Clara County, San Jose has participated in and benefited from the booming electronics and computer-related economy that has been created by Silicon Valley's high-tech businesses. Photo by Chromosohm/Sohm

and grown within a few weeks into large sheets. These are then surgically applied to the injured area to repair it.

Dr. David Woodley, who leads this group, recently succeeded in cloning a special type of collagen, Type 7. By inserting this gene into individual cells, skin tissue can be developed with immunity to a rare genetic blistering disease.

• *the nerve chip*: A Stanford research group has implanted a "nerve chip" into rats that incorporates living nerve tissue into a silicon microchip. That microchip could someday produce a bionic artificial limb that communicates electronically with the human nervous system.

• *genetic engineering*: While many researchers have contributed to the development of genetic

achieved rapid successes by producing approaches to treating viral diseases and AIDS.

Stanford researchers have also made important contributions in nonscientific areas, including, among many others:

• *measurement of intelligence*: Psychologist Louis M. Terman helped develop the Stanford-Binet test for individual IQ, a test now in its fourth edition. Terman's study of 1,528 intellectually gifted children debunked many myths concerning the impairments and neurotic behavior of people with superior intellectual qualities and characteristics.

• *principles of practical economics*: Kenneth Arrow received the Nobel Prize for his contributions to the general economic equilibrium theory as well as welfare economics. Arrow's ideas

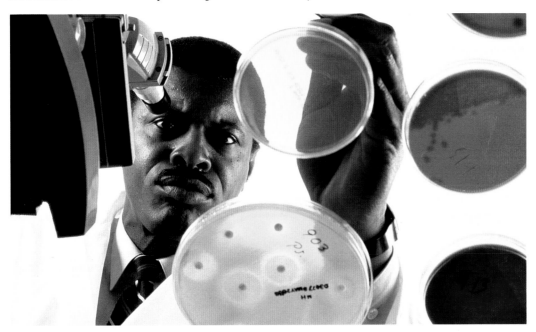

Genetic engineering is just one field being tackled by the researchers of the region's educational institutions. Photo by Pete Saloutos/The Photo File

engineering, it was molecular geneticists Stanley Cohen of Stanford and Herbert Boyer of the University of California at San Francisco who made it practical. They showed how human DNA can be inserted into the genetic machinery of bacterial cells and made to function. Bacteria with human genetic information can churn out large quantities of man's own body chemicals, allowing for the treatment of diseases with drugs nature expressly intended for the purpose.

Cohen and Boyer's research has not only enabled the study of genes at an entirely new level, it has also sparked the development of the nascent biotechnology industry, including such companies as Amgen, Biogen, KNAX, Genentech, Intelligenetics, Regeneron and others. Some of these biotech firms have

form the basis for most of the principles and ideals applied to practical economics, and they are credited with contributing to a higher standard of living and to fuller employment in industrialized nations.

• *computer-aided teaching* (1966): Philosophy professor Patrick Suppes and Richard Atkinson introduced the concept of computer-aided instruction and its possibilities for education. Students at Brentwood Elementary School in East Palo Alto were among the first in the nation to learn by computer.

Suppes' ideas have become the main force in developing computer programs and teaching aids for all levels of education across the U.S. He is the recipient of the National Medal of Science for his educational contributions to the nation.

▲ UNIVERSITY OF CALIFORNIA AT BERKELEY

The University of California at Berkeley is known internationally for the strength and breadth of its research. In a recent national survey of the reputations of graduate programs by the Conference Board of Associated Research Councils, Berkeley was ranked in the top 10 in 30 out of 32 fields—far more than any other university in the country.

The UC Berkeley campus overlooks the San Francisco Bay and the Golden Gate Bridge from the foothills of the East Bay in one of America's most lively, culturally diverse and politically adventurous cities. Its student population totals approximately 31,000, including graduates and undergraduates. The university takes pride in maintaining a multiethnic, multicultural student body.

The University of California established a campus at Berkeley in 1873 with an enrollment of 191 students. Contrary to the practice of the time, the university's founders decided the school would not be church-affiliated. After initially excluding women, Berkeley's Board of Regents opened the university's doors to students of both sexes.

By the 1920s UC Berkeley had become the world's largest university, with just over 14,000 full-time students, but it had yet to achieve its international reputation and was still regarded primarily as a regional institution. That changed when a graduate physicist from Yale, Ernest O. Lawrence, chose to pursue his academic career at Berkeley. In 1939 Lawrence became the first person from a state university to win the Nobel Prize (for his work in physics). He eventually helped to bring to Berkeley a group of outstanding chemists and physicists and establish a facility that would become one of the world's leading centers for research and education: the Lawrence Berkeley Laboratory.

In 1940 the Rockefeller Foundation pledged $1.4 million to Lawrence and the university toward the development of the 184-inch Cyclotron. This device, later redesigned and renamed the synchrocyclotron, played an important role in the early study of mesons—particles involved in the strong subatomic force. During World War II the cyclotron was used in the Manhattan Project, which produced the atomic bomb.

Today the Lawrence Berkeley Laboratory (LBL) is administered by the University of California for the U.S. Department of Energy (DOE) and continues to be a major resource to more than 200 faculty members and 700 graduate students who use its facilities to conduct research in the physical and life sciences.

The University of California at Berkeley, with more than 2,000 research projects under way, has an international reputation as one of the world's leading research universities. The U.C. Berkeley faculty can proudly boast 11 Nobel Laureates, 93 members of the National Academy of Sciences, 57 members of the National Academy of Engineering, and 99 members of the Academy of Arts and Sciences. Photo by Kerrick James

In response to national needs, LBL conducts research in such fields as physics, chemistry, engineering and materials science. The laboratory was recently selected as one of the nation's high-temperature superconductivity research centers and as a major site for DOE's role in the Human Genome Project, designed to decipher the entire human genetic blueprint, with major benefits expected in health and basic biology.

UC Berkeley holds a commanding reputation among the world's leading research universities, with more than 2,000 research projects currently underway. These projects range from identifying cancer-causing substances in the environment to developing artificial intelligence as a tool to expand human knowledge and creativity.

The UC Berkeley faculty of approximately 1,500 includes 11 Nobel Laureates, 93 members of the National Academy of Sciences, 57 members of the National Academy of Engineering and 99 members of the American Academy of Arts and Sciences. With the award of a Nobel Prize in Chemistry to Professor Yuan T. Lee in 1986, UC Berkeley became the leading university in the country in the number of Nobel Laureates on its faculty. (At last count, Stanford had 10; Harvard 9; M.I.T. 7.) UC Berkeley also continues to be the nation's leading producer of Ph.D.'s and leads in the number of undergraduates who ultimately win Ph.D.'s.

UC Berkeley researchers have contributed significantly to scientific knowledge in a wide range of fields. The university's contributions include, among many others:

• *the Ames test*: Developed by Bruce Ames, this is a simple and inexpensive system for detecting mutagens (chemicals that damage DNA) and potential carcinogens. The test has set the world standard for detecting natural and man-made substances with cancer-causing potential and has allowed many potentially dangerous products to be detected and altered before they went on the market.

• *high-energy physics*: Invention of the cyclotron at Berkeley made the campus a leading center in developing the science of high-energy physics, thus contributing to the opening of the Atomic Age. The cyclotron and other atomic accelerators at Berkeley, along with the development of the bubble chamber to track accelerated atomic particles, opened the way for major advances in

understanding the fundamental structure of matter. The Bevatron, for example, was used in the discovery of the antiproton, confirming the existence of antimatter.

• *nuclear physics*: Nuclear research at Berkeley led to the discovery of 16 new chemical elements, including plutonium and all other known transuranium elements.

• *molecular clock*: Berkeley's Vincent Sarich and Allan Wilson pioneered efforts to measure evolutionary relationships between animals by comparing the chemical makeup of their genes.

• *growth studies*: The Institute for Human Development at Berkeley is the longest-running longitudinal study of personality and emotional development in the United States. Begun in 1928, the study has systematically followed several hundred San Francisco Bay Area residents from childhood through middle age and is now following them into their retirement.

• *science education*: The Lawrence Hall of Science is a major center for research, development and teacher training in science education at elementary, high school and junior college levels. The center's Chem Study Project developed a modern new course in high school chemistry, now in thousands of high schools around the U.S. and other countries. The Science Curriculum Improvement Study continues to develop methods and materials for introducing science in a valid way to young children in primary grades.

• *viruses*: Berkeley's Virus Laboratory achieved the first isolation and crystallization of a virus affecting man and animals (human polio virus); the first successful experiment taking a virus apart and putting it together again, thus showing that nucleic acid controls both reproduction and infectivity; and is currently contributing notable advances in understanding the relationship between viruses and cancer.

• *biological control of crop pests*: Much of the science of biological control of crop pests was first developed at Berkeley, including the idea of using insect disease pathogens to fight insect pests.

Since the mid-1980s the UC Berkeley campus has been selected by the National Science Foundation to launch a number of new centers to promote basic research and at the same time speed the transfer of technology to both the public and private sectors. These include:

• *Center for Massive Information Storage and Retrieval*: This center was established at the university in 1988 to develop the technology needed to sort, store and make full use of the vast on-line capacities of modern computers. Nearly all of UC Berkeley's computer science faculty and many graduate students will contribute to the research carried on there.

• *Center for Cell Morphology and Function*: Faculty scientists working at this center are helping develop a new generation of imaging devices for studying nerve growth, nerve impulses and other vital biological processes in real time.

• *Center for Plant Development Biology Research*: Researchers at this center identify plant genes responsible for crop productivity and disease resistance and explore ways to assure desired genes are "expressed" when and where they will have the greatest benefit.

• *Plant Gene Expression Center*: Recognizing the quality of plant science at UC Berkeley, the U.S. Department of Agriculture established the center in 1984 in partnership with the university. Berkeley plant molecular biologists head many research projects at the center, which is located in the USDA's Agricultural Research Service facilities in Albany, near the campus. One of the center's early successes was the use of a kind of high-speed gun to "shoot" tungsten particles coated with genetic materials into living plant tissue. This development

is expected to provide a practical means of transferring desired genes to cereal crops.

• *Center for Particle Astrophysics*: This center draws on the talents of faculty scientists and engineers as well as the campus Space Sciences Laboratory and Radio Astronomy Laboratory. The adjacent Lawrence Berkeley Laboratory also plays a major role. The center's initial mission is to better understand "dark matter"—thought to make up more than 90 percent of the mass of the universe, but nearly undetectable. The center couples theo-

reticians with campus and LBL experimenters who develop hypersensitive radiation sensors. If past astronomy spin-offs are any guide, these new sensors should ultimately advance medical imaging technology and remote satellite sensing.

• *Sensor Actuator Center.* Berkeley's Industry Visitors Program allows industrial sponsors to have one of their own researchers work alongside university faculty and graduate students for four months at a time at this NSF-funded center. Faculty and graduate students at the center have recently demonstrated that extraordinarily small mechanical devices can be manufactured using materials and fabrication methods already in place in the semiconductor industry. Some see this new development as the next revolution in the industry.

Since its establishment in the last century, Berkeley has dealt with so-called technology transfer through publications of individual scientific and technical research results and the patenting or licensing of inventions. Berkeley's contributions have run the gamut from soil fumigation practices vital to the $400-million California strawberry industry to development of a patented silicon chip that converts analog signals to digital, now used in telecommunications worldwide.

More than 60 patents have been issued for Berkeley inventions during the last 20 years; more than 40 commercial licenses are currently in effect in the chemical and engineering fields, electronics and biosciences, to name a few.

▲ University of California at San Francisco

The University of California at San Francisco is one of the largest and most modern health sciences facilities on the West Coast. The only one of the nine UC campuses devoted solely to the this field, UCSF is a recognized leader in health sciences education, research and clinical care.

UCSF was first established in 1873 when the San Francisco-based Toland Medical College and the California College of Pharmacy agreed to affiliate with the University of California (at Berkeley across the bay). Schools of dentistry and nursing were added in 1881 and 1907, respectively.

In 1895 Adolph Sutro donated 13 acres of land on a hill overlooking Golden Gate Park to UCSF. A year later the Affiliated Colleges, as they were then called, opened the doors of their new Parnassus Heights campus.

The first UCSF campus facility actually built for use as a hospital was finished in 1917. A clinics building to offer outpatient dental and medical care to the community was constructed in 1934. The newest addition to the UCSF campus, a four-story structure and grounds in Laurel Heights, was acquired in 1985.

In 1991 more than 2,500 students attended the UCSF schools of dentistry, medicine, nursing, pharmacy and graduate academic programs, including some 1,250 students and scholars from 68 countries. The school maintains a full- and part-time staff of nearly 13,000 teachers, clinicians and other personnel.

UCSF's outpatient service is one of the largest in California. Several hundred physicians on the attending staff and clinical faculty treat thousands of patients each year at the three hospitals that make up the school's Medical Center: Moffitt, Long and Langley Porter Psychiatric Hospital. Major UCSF-affiliated programs are also in place at San Francisco General Hospital and the Veteran Administration Medical Center.

UCSF enjoys a dazzling reputation for pioneering research in fields of study ranging from molecular genetics

First established in 1873, the University of California at San Francisco (UCSF) is the only one of nine UC campuses devoted exclusively to health sciences. Photo by Gerald L. French/The Photo File

to care for the elderly and from immune-system disorders to tooth decay. Among the many health science research accomplishments at UCSF are the following:

• *Biotechnology*: Much of the work at UCSF has been revolutionized by the use of "gene splicing" techniques—techniques that were spawned 15 years ago when UCSF biochemist Herbert Boyer and his Stanford collaborator, Stanley Cohen, first developed the recombinant DNA technique and used it to turn bacteria into protein "factories."

This discovery has since been used at UCSF and elsewhere to artificially create such substances as human growth hormone, human insulin, interferon, interleukin II, tissue plasminogen factor (TPA) and hepatitis B vaccine. In fact, of the handful of such therapeutic products now approved for human use by the FDA, three—human growth hormone, hepatitis B vaccine, and human insulin—emerged from UCSF laboratories.

The close juxtaposition of clinicians, clinical researchers and basic scientists at UCSF has made such developments possible. Among the school's other research developments are:

• *canning industry standards*: Karl F. Meyer, an early UC San Francisco medical researcher, helped save the California canning industry from the threat of botulism and established the standards upon which the industry based its safety standards. He also isolated the virus that causes Western equine encephalitis, discovered that plague resides naturally in the state's wild rodent population and identified the bacteria that causes shellfish poisoning.

• *treatment for pernicious anemia*: George Whipple won the Nobel Prize (elsewhere) in 1934 for work he started at UCSF that led to the discovery of a treatment for pernicious anemia.

• *discovery of vitamin E*: Herbert Evans discovered Vitamin E (alpha-tocopheral) in the 1920s. He also discovered animal growth hormone and developed what came to be known as "Evans blue," a blood dye technique used throughout the

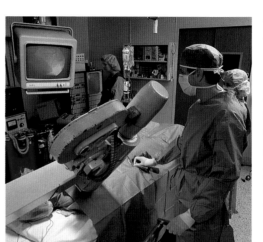

world to measure blood volume.

• *human growth hormone*: Biochemist Choh Hao Li was the first to isolate and purify six of the seven hormones produced in the human pituitary gland. In 1966 Li determined the structure of human growth hormone and synthesized it for the first time in 1971. He discovered or isolated numerous other hormones, including beta endorphin in 1975.

Thanks largely to the pioneering work of Dr. Li, John Baxter and colleagues were able to clone the gene for human growth hormone in 1979, a feat that led to its genetically engineered production by Genentech and eventual FDA approval. UCSF participated in the national clinical trials that preceded this approval.

Today injection of synthetic growth hormone has helped thousands of children achieve their normal height by replacing what their own pituitary glands failed to produce.

• *the Pap Smear test*: Gynecological pathologist Herbert F. Traut, who teamed up with George Papanicolaou at Cornell University from 1939 to 1942 to perfect the test and show that it could reliably detect cancers of the cervix, uterus and vagina, came to UCSF in 1942 to continue his efforts. As co-developer of the test and chairman of obstetrics and gynecology, he presided over a special laboratory funded by the American Cancer Society to perform large-scale testing and encourage routine use of the test by physicians.

• *genetically engineered human vaccine*: In 1981 William Rutter, director of the Hormone Research Laboratory, cloned the gene for the outer coat of the hepatitis B virus and inserted it into bacteria. Chiron Corporation, which Rutter co-founded, refined the technique to obtain the protein in quantity and brought it to market in 1986 as the world's first genetically engineered human vaccine.

• *prenatal diagnosis*: This field was pioneered by UCSF physicians and surgeons. Yuet Wain Kan developed the molecular techniques and Mitchell Golbus the clinical techniques that allowed the first fetal test in 1976, which identified sickle cell anemia as well as other genetic blood diseases, including thalassemia—a test Kan also developed—and have opened up the possibility of treating the fetus while still in the womb.

Golbus and associates also have done the definitive work proving amniocentesis and, later, chorionic villus sampling, safe and accurate for in utero diagnostic procedures.

• *fetal surgery.* Golbus and pediatric surgeon Michael Harrison performed the first successful in utero surgical procedure in 1981. Only 10 days later Harrison and Golbus became the first to partially remove a fetus from the mother for surgery.

• *organ transplants.* The kidney transplant team at UCSF has performed more kidney transplants than any other group in the world (3,700 as of early 1991). The team has made numerous contributions to transplant surgery. They were the first to show that the chances of organ rejection could be greatly diminished by a series of three blood transfusions from the organ donor before surgery. They also developed a system that made it possible to expand the use of cadaver donor kidneys. The system, now used at centers throughout the world, allows surgeons to preserve the organ for up to 72 hours, making it possible to recover donor organs from more distant hospitals for transplantation.

• *AIDS research.* UCSF clinicians and researchers were among the first in the nation to recognize the danger of AIDS and to warn about its far-reaching effects. They set up the first outpatient clinic and inpatient ward in the country at UCSF-affiliated San Francisco General Hospital and mounted an enormous, multidisciplinary effort to fight AIDS, both locally and nationally, long before there was any grant money available.

Today some 300 UCSF researchers and clinicians at the Parnassus campus, San Francisco General, and Veterans Administration Medical Center are working in a variety of specialties in the fight against this deadly disease. Their projects cover a broad range, from the epidemiology of how AIDS is spread to developing a model for care that is both humane and cost effective, and includes preventive public health education and basic studies of the AIDS virus and the immune system.

Jay Levy's laboratory at UCSF was the source of many firsts in the attack on the AIDS virus. It was one of the first research groups in the world to isolate the AIDS virus.

The group collaborated in the first cloning and the first sequencing of ARV virus with three other research groups and with Chiron Corporation of Emeryville. These developments allowed the determination of the structure of the viral genes.

The group was the first to isolate the virus from cerebrospinal fluid, intestinal tissue and vaginal secretions. It established that the standard treatment of blood-derived clotting factors used by hemophiliacs does not kill the AIDS virus, but that heat treatment of these factors does.

UCSF dermatologist Marcus Conant, in collaboration with Levy's lab, first established that latex condoms are an effective barrier to the AIDS virus.

UCSF pediatric immunologists were the first to warn the Centers for Disease Control in Atlanta in 1982 that blood transfusions could transmit the disease after they found a 20-month-old baby who had contracted the disease from transfusions in UCSF hospitals after birth.

Directed by a university-wide task force, UCSF School of Dentistry researchers set up the first tissue bank—now the world's largest repository of AIDS tissue specimens—to study causes of the disease.

Early in the epidemic, UCSF physicians at San Francisco General were the first to develop infection-control guidelines to protect AIDS patients and hospital workers who deal with them. Subsequently reported in the *New England Journal of Medicine*, these guidelines have been widely utilized around the country.

UCSF's reputation for research excellence continues to grow in scope and significance. The campus attracts more National Institutes of Health research funds than almost any other institution in the country, and young scientists in biology seem to be flocking to UCSF to conduct the basic research and clinical studies that precede medical breakthroughs.

According to a recent survey, American universities conduct about two-thirds of all the research in the U.S. At Stanford federal support for research has grown to an annual level of $240 million. The total value of contracts and grants at UC Berkeley has exceeded $210 million. Private corporations also continue to support campus science and engineering research, which is essential for long-range industrial growth but requires more time than industry can usually afford on its own.

NORTHERN CALIFORNIA COLLEGES AND UNIVERSITIES

RIGHT: Local students take advantage of the many fine Bay Area institutions of higher learning. Photo by Chromosohm/ Sohm

▲ Academy of Art College (San Francisco): four-year proprietary art college, coed

▲ Armstrong College (Berkeley): four-year proprietary business college, coed

▲ California College of Arts and Crafts (Oakland): four-year art college, coed

▲ California Maritime Academy (Vallejo): four-year maritime academy, coed

▲ California State University, Hayward: four-year public university, coed

▲ Canada College (Redwood City): two-year public community college, coed

▲ City College of San Francisco: two-year public community college, coed

▲ Cogswell Polytechnical College (Cupertino): four-year private technical college, coed

▲ College of Alameda: two-year public community college, coed

▲ College of Marin, Kentfield: two-year public community college, coed

▲ College of Notre Dame (Belmont): four-year private liberal arts college, coed, affiliated with the Roman Catholic Church

▲ College of San Mateo: two-year public community college, coed

▲ Contra Costa College (San Pablo): two-year public community college, coed

▲ De Anza College (Cupertino): two-year public community college, coed

▲ Diablo Valley College (Pleasant Hill): two-year public community college, coed

▲ Dominican College of San Rafael: four-year private liberal arts college, affiliated with Roman Catholic Church

▲ Dominican School of Philosophy and Theology (Berkeley): two-year upper-division private seminary college, coed, affiliated with Roman Catholic Church

▲ Evergreen Valley College (San Jose): two-year public community college, coed

▲ California Fashion Institute of Design and Merchandising (San Francisco): two-year proprietary art, junior college, coed

▲ Foothill College (Los Altos Hills): two-year public community college, coed

▲ Golden Gate University (San Francisco): four-year private university, coed

▲ Heald Business College, Rohnert Park: one-year private business college, coed

▲ Heald Business College, San Jose: two-year private business college, coed

▲ Heald Business College, Walnut Creek: two-year private business college, coed

▲ Heald Institute of Technology (Martinez): two-year private technical college, coed

▲ Holy Names College (Oakland): four-year private liberal arts college, coed, affiliated with Roman Catholic Church

▲ John F. Kennedy University (Orinda): two-year upper-division private liberal arts college, coed

▲ Laney College (Oakland): two-year public community college, coed

▲ Lincoln University (San Francisco): four-year private university and business, liberal arts college, coed

▲ Los Medanos College (Pittsburg): two-year public community college, coed.

▲ Louise Salinger Academy of Fashion (San Francisco): four-year private school of fashion, coed

▲ Menlo College (Atherton): four-year private college of arts and sciences, coed

▲ Merritt College (Oakland): two-year public community college, coed

▲ Mills College (Oakland): four-year private liberal arts college, women only

▲ Mission College (Santa Clara): two-year public community college, coed

▲ Napa Valley College (Napa): two-year public community college, coed.

▲ National Hispanic University (San Jose): four-year private business, liberal arts, teachers college, coed

▲ New College of California (San Francisco): four-year private alternative humanities college, coed

▲ Ohlone College (Fremont): two-year public community college, coed

▲ Pacific Union College (Angwin): four-year private liberal arts college, coed, affiliated with Seventh-day Adventists

▲ Patten College (Oakland): four-year private Bible college, coed, affiliated with Christian Evangelical Churches of America

▲ Phillips Junior College, Condi Campus (Campbell): two-year proprietary junior, technical college, coed

▲ Queen of the Holy Rosary College (Fremont): two-year private seminary college, women only, affiliated with Roman Catholic Church

▲ St. Joseph's College Seminary (Mountain View): four-year private seminary college, men only, affiliated with Roman Catholic Church

▲ St. Mary's College of California (Moraga): four-year private liberal arts college, coed, affiliated with Roman Catholic Church

▲ Samuel Merritt College (Oakland): four-year private nursing college coed

▲ San Francisco Art Institute: four-year private art college, coed

▲ San Francisco College of Mortuary Science: one-year private technical college, coed

▲ San Francisco Conservatory of Music: four-year private music college, coed

▲ San Francisco State University: four-year public university, coed

A Santa Clara University law student heads to class. Photo by Chromosohm/Sohm

▲ San Jose Christian College: four-year private Bible college, coed interdenominational

▲ San Jose City College: two-year public community college, coed

▲ San Jose State University: four-year public university and liberal arts college, coed

▲ Santa Clara University: four-year private university, coed, affiliated with Roman Catholic Church

▲ Santa Rosa Junior College: two-year public community junior college, coed

▲ Skyline College (San Bruno): two-year public community college, coed

▲ Solano Community College (Suisun City): two-year public community college, coed

▲ Sonoma State University (Rohnert Park): four-year public university, coed

▲ Stanford University (Rohnert Park): four-year public university, coed

▲ Stanford University (Palo Alto): four-year private university, coed

▲ University of California, Berkeley: four-year public university, coed

▲ University of California, San Francisco: two-year upper division public university, coed

▲ University of San Francisco: four-year private university, coed, affiliated with Roman Catholic Church

▲ Vista Community College (Berkeley): two-year public community college, coed.

▲ West Valley College (Saratoga): two-year public community college, coed

▲ World College West (Petaluma): four-year private liberal arts college, coed.

Ivy decorates the campus buildings of San Jose State University in Santa Clara County. Photo by Gerald L. French/The Photo File

GETTING DOWN TO BUSINESS

By Art Garcia

he Bay Area's "anything goes" mentality helps make it particular-ly appealing to innovators and entrepreneurs, those modern-day discoverers and charters of business and scientific territories previously unknown.

Dating back to the days of Levi Strauss and Leland Stan-ford, the Bay Area has been a region of entrepreneurial pioneering and innovation. Photo by Chris Springmann/ The Photo File

❑ ❑ ❑

San Francisco workers take a break from the busy workday at Embarcadero Center. Photo by Bob Rowan/Progressive Image

▲ ENTREPRENEURS AND INNOVATORS

"California has recaptured what America once had, the spirit of pioneering," said department store founder and San Franciscan, the late Cyril Magnin. High-tech industry executives would add that the state still is the frontier, just substitute computers for land. In their book *California Inc.*, journalists Joel Kotkin and Paul Grabowicz noted that for California, more than any other state, economic growth has been linked to people with big ideas. Few were native sons and almost all were lured by the chance to get things done.

The Bay Area boasts an impressive list of entrepreneurs and innovators: railroad magnates Mark Hopkins and Leland Stanford, Bank of America founder A.P. Giannini, 1850s dry-goods salesman Levi Strauss, contractors Henry J. Kaiser and Warren Bechtel, electronics pioneers William Hewlett and David Packard, transistor inventor William Shockley, and the co-founders of Apple Computer, Inc., Steven Wozniak and Steven Jobs.

Much of the Bay Area's business heart is pumped by services such as capital formation, banking, finance, tourism and retail, and most of the region's industry, including semiconductor and computer manufacturing, electronics, aerospace, and biotechnology, is of the clean variety.

▲ VENTURE CAPITALISTS

Look behind the entrepreneurial success stories of such corporate names as Apple Computer and Federal Express, back to their formative and developmental stages of growth and venture capitalists (VCs) almost always turn up. They often finance small, privately held businesses in exchange for stock. Frequently VCs provide management talent as well as capital to emerging companies.

Menlo Park in San Mateo County has become the home of an extraordinary number of venture capital firms. Their business park address, 3000 Sand Hill Road, was designed especially for these firms and has become synonymous with America's venture capital core. Nearby is Silicon Valley, the premiere breeding ground for the prime targets of most venture capital firms when 3000 Sand Hill was developed.

To be sure, not all the major venture capital players are located along Sand Hill Road. Palo Alto and San Francisco also have their concentrations of VC firms that supply seed money and management support to companies of all kinds in the Bay Area's spawning pool for entrepreneurial ventures. More than 40 venture capital firms operate from Menlo Park and more than one-fifth of the nation's top venture capitalists are headquartered in the Bay Area.

Venture capital is a powerful economic force, with at least 3,000 venture capitalists with more than $30 billion at their disposal competing for entrepreneurial investments. Venture capital is one of the key advantages the U.S. has in holding its technological lead in the world marketplace, a system that is the envy of Europe and Asia. Venture capital grew up in America, but it was born in the Bay Area.

▲ FINANCIAL CENTER

Though no longer recognized as the financial center of the West, San Francisco today remains a booming financial center. Two of California's three largest banks, Bank of America and Wells Fargo, have made San Francisco their home from their first days. Also headquartered in the city are the 12th District Federal Reserve Bank, which serves nine western states, and the Federal Home Loan Bank of San Francisco, whose district includes California, Arizona and Nevada. The biggest of the nation's 12 district banks, it contains some of the largest savings institutions in the country. Virtually all of the major foreign banks have offices in San Francisco, and many foreign companies have chosen the city as their beachhead in the U.S. market.

The Pacific Stock Exchange, the nation's largest regional marketplace for securities, began its long history in the late nineteenth century in San Francisco, where it maintains a fully operational trading floor as a co-site

with a Los Angeles floor. Now nearing its 65th year in business, Transamerica Corporation, incorporated by A.P. Giannini to own Bank of America's stock, is a full-range provider of specialized financial and insurance services whose pyramid headquarters building is a downtown San Francisco landmark.

In addition, more than 70 investment houses are located in the city, including the nation's largest discount brokerage, San Francisco-based Charles Schwab & Company.

The Pacific Stock Exchange is the nation's largest regional marketplace for securities. It maintains a fully operational trading floor as a co-site with a Los Angeles floor. Photos by Amy Seidman-Tighe

▲ BUSINESS SERVICES

The Bay Area hosts an impressive number of business-service firms as well. While San Francisco is an attractive center for law, accounting and consulting firms, it is Contra Costa County that has developed into the region's corridor of business services. The Contra Costa Council predicts services, the county's largest industry division, accounted for more than half of expected job growth in 1990, adding 10,000 jobs to the local economy. Business services are the largest and consistently the most rapidly growing segment of the services sector.

Fueling the fast growth of business services are the greater use and applications of computers and a trend by large companies to contract out for services that before had been performed internally. The Contra Costa Council expects these trends to continue stimulating demand for specialized technology-related business services, such as computer and data-processing services, research and development laboratories, management consultants and public relations and advertising firms.

Other professional services, including legal and the grouping of engineering, architecture, research and accounting, are forecast for additional growth by the Council. They are being fed by the steady flow of major companies in San Francisco and Oakland that are opening offices in Contra Costa County and other firms expand in response to the county's healthy corporate presence.

FACING PAGE:
Transamerica Corporation, in business for more than half a century, provides a full range of specialized financial and insurance services. Its corporate headquarters projects a distinct image in the San Francisco skyline. Photo by Bob Rowan/Progressive Image

Bay Area commuters head home after a busy day's work. Photo by Ed Young/The Photo File

The manufacture and testing of computer hardware has developed as a result of a more diversified and high-tech economy in the Bay Area.
Photo by Mark E. Gibson

▲ HEALTH SERVICES

Health services account for Contra Costa's second-largest service industry and will grow at an above-average rate in the early 1990s, while the county's other service industries will also see brisk growth. Among them are child care centers, part of social services, which have become a staple in and near new office parks along the 690 corridor. Commercial developers are promoting these centers as an important business amenity. With hotels moving in to match the corridor's expansion, the hotel industry books continued employee growth as well.

▲ ART AS BUSINESS

Among the region's entertainment industry firms are Lucasfilms Ltd., in Marin County, Northern California's largest film company; the Saul Zaentz Company Film Center and Fantasy Records in Berkeley (Alameda County); One Pass Video in San Francisco; and Concord Jazz in Concord (Contra Costa County).

The Bay Area is second only to New York City as host to the largest number of independent presses in the United States and as a center of architectural design, with one of every six practicing U.S. architects maintaining an office in the Bay Area.

Another growing Bay Area design-service business is fashion design and production, especially casual ready-to-wear and children's apparel. Local wholesale marts that market products of designers are San Francisco's Showplace Square, Contract Design Center, Gift Center, San Francisco Apparel Mart and the recently opened San Francisco Fashion Center.

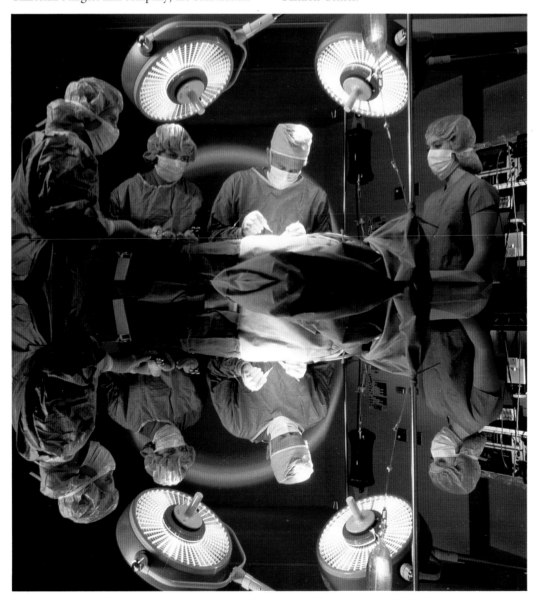

The health services industry in the Bay Area is predicted to grow at an above-average rate in the 1990s. Photo by Pete Saloutos/The Photo File

▲ TOURISM

Tourism is big business in the Bay Area with more than 13 million visitors a year flocking to San Francisco and spending $4 billion (revenue that generates direct employment for more than 60,000 workers). A recent poll in Condé-Nast's *Traveler* magazine revealed that readers rated the city the most popular destination in the world, passing Paris for the first time.

More and more visitors are leaving their hearts in San Francisco, with Japanese tourists being the highest rollers among them, not only in San Francisco and the Greater Bay Area, but also in California. A third of the city's 26,000 hotel rooms were booked by international visitors in 1989, half from Europe and a third from Japan and Southeast Asia.

In an area filled with scenic and recreational attractions, even more are in the works or in planning stages to make the Bay Area a still greater draw for conventions and exhibits. Moscone Convention Center has been expanded to add rooftop meeting rooms, while a north exhibit hall was completed in May 1992. The additions increased the capacity to 585,000 square feet of usable space, from 350,000 square feet.

Across the street is the long talked about, often delayed, but still scheduled $1.5-billion Yerba Buena Center, an 87-acre development adjacent to San Francisco's downtown office and retail core. The largest planned building program in the city's history includes an already completed 1,500-room hotel and the new home of the Museum of Modern Art. Planned are a million square feet of office space, 200,000 square feet of retail, 1,700 underground parking spaces and 500 housing units. Also being considered are an outdoor ice rink, nightclub and health club.

RIGHT: San Francisco is a favorite destination of Asian travelers, with a third of the city's 26,000 hotel rooms booked by Japanese and Southeast Asians. Photo by Chromosohm/Sohm

BELOW: Tourism is big business in the Bay Area. With more than 17 million visitors each year flocking to San Francisco, the city is now the most alluring destination in the world. Photo by Chromosohm/ Sohm

A 1989 survey commissioned by the San Francisco Convention and Visitors Bureau found that the six things about the city most enjoyed by visitors remained constant from prior years: weather topped the list, followed by people, scenery/views, food/restaurants, atmosphere/ambience, and shopping. In the most recent survey, 92 percent of respondents reported "very high" satisfaction with their trips to San Francisco.

Of course, a good deal of that satisfaction comes from enjoying the other parts of the Bay Area's vast vacationland, where visitors essentially can find the best creations of nature and man's imagination. With an ideal climate with an average annual temperature variation of less than 10 degrees, San Mateo County is a popular area for vacations and conventions. There are more than 100 hotels and motels with more than 11,000 rooms, plus another 1,500 rooms being added through new construction. The Cow Palace exhibit facility, San Mateo Expo Center, and the Circle Star Theater support the county's tourism and business-service base.

Touring Napa Valley from a hot-air balloon is a special treat for visitors to the famous wine country. Charming bed-and-breakfasts dot the countryside, providing a unique travel experience to even the most jaded tourist. Photo by Mark E. Gibson

When planned expansions are completed in 1992, the Moscone Convention Center will feature some 600,000 square feet of usable space. Photo by Gerald L. French/The Photo File

▲ CONSUMER MARKET

The Bay Area maintains a disproportionate share, relative to its size, of California's personal income, the highest of any state. Its nine counties, with a population of more than 6 million, comprise one of the wealthiest regions in America. By the year 2000 the Bay Area will have the state's top five counties with the highest per capita income, led by Marin County at $28,381. Marin, which currently leads California in average household income at $73,412, will see that average rise to nearly $86,400 at the beginning of the new century, followed by San Mateo County's $73,200. This buying power spills over to an abundant life-style, heavy consumer purchases of soft and hard goods, and broad investments in recreation and entertainment.

Santa Clara County, sparked by the San Jose metropolitan area, is fourth in the nation in median household effective buying income at more than $42,000. San Jose now is the 11th-largest city in the U.S. and third largest in California, leapfrogging San Francisco in the late 1980s to that position (behind Los Angeles and San Diego). Even more significant are the following statistics: The Greater San Jose area is fourth in the nation in percentage (40.2 percent) of households with incomes of $50,000 or more.

San Mateo County, with a population of more than 723,959 and a total effective buying income approaching $13 billion, is one of California's more affluent and attractive markets. It ranks second in the state in per capita income and second in per household income. The county's per capita income of nearly $22,430 is nearly 29 percent higher than the state average and a bit more than 7 percent above the average of other Bay Area counties.

▲ THE RETAIL SECTOR

As one of the nation's wealthiest regions, the Bay Area is recognized as a major retail market. San Francisco and San Mateo County offer examples of the area's retail sector.

An internationally known retail industry is clustered around downtown San Francisco's Union Square, serving the sophisticated and trendsetting tastes of Bay Area shoppers through prestige-name American and foreign department stores, shops, and boutiques. The opening of San Francisco Centre in late 1988 increased the city's retailing concentration within the quarter-mile radius of

Union Square. A spiral escalator built in Japan, the first of its kind in the U.S., carries shoppers around 130 specialty shops on five floors and to the upper levels of a major, upscale department store.

Embarcadero Center, Ghirardelli Square and The Cannery, all located near or along the Bay, are popular shopping and dining destinations for tourists and Bay Area residents. Many of San Francisco's neighborhoods have their own unique shopping districts, among them are Union Street, Polk Street, The Haight, upper Market Street, the Mission and The Castro.

Shoppers in San Mateo County have a wide selection of retail outlets, including five regional shopping centers and 100 other community, neighborhood and downtown shopping areas. This broad range of services and merchandise adds up to a retail sales market that is number one in California. Major shopping complexes are Hillsdale and Fashion Island Center in San Mateo, Serramonte and Westlake in Daly City, and Tanforan in San Bruno.

ABOVE: Sausalito stores, with their handcrafted gifts, make shopping a pleasurable experience for visitors to the picturesque hamlet of Marin County. Photo by Chromosohm/ Sohm

FACING PAGE: Ghirardelli Square is a favorite retail destination for both residents and tourists. Photo by Gerald L. French/The Photo File

▲ CORPORATE HEADQUARTERS

Until the end of World War II, San Francisco was the manufacturing, distribution and trade center of the West. After the war other regional economic centers matured and the Bay Area became the fourth-largest metropolitan market in the country. In the 1980s, during the nation's rush to corporate restructuring, nearly half of San Francisco's *Fortune* 500 corporate headquarters offices were lost. Despite the losses, San Francisco still plays a significant role as a corporate headquarters city but shares a small part of that status with other Bay Area cities. As most of the migration to California from elsewhere in the nation and overseas has funneled into Southern California, the tilt of business and finance has followed the crowd and, similarly, has shifted to Los Angeles and environs.

Yet more than 50 corporate giants headquartered in the Bay Area and representing a wide diversity of industries were included in a recent *Business Week 1000,* a list of America's most valuable companies. These corporations, grouped here geographically by county and city, include:

ALAMEDA COUNTY

Berkeley XOMA (drugs and research) *Emeryville* Chiron (drugs and research) *Oakland* American President Companies (shipping) The Clorox Company (consumer products, personal care) Dreyer's Grand Ice Cream (food processing) Golden West Financial (savings and loan) Safeway Stores (food retailing)

CONTRA COSTA COUNTY

Concord Tosco (oil and gas)

MARIN COUNTY

Sausalito Autodesk (computer software and services)

SAN FRANCISCO

Bankamerica (bank)—listed in *Business Week's* "Top 15 in Assets" Charles Schwab (financial services)

FACING PAGE: San Francisco's Embarcadero Center provides a unique downtown shopping and dining experience. Photo by Ed Young/The Photo File

The Bank of America Processing Center in Concord is one of many industries that has made Contra Costa County the region's corridor of business services. Photo by Bob Rowan/Progressive Image

Home to more than 50 corporate giants, the Bay Area provides abundant economic opportunities—from banking and finance to electronics and pharmaceuticals. Photo by Gerald L. French/The Photo File

Chevron (oil and gas)—listed in *Business Week's* "Top 15 in Market Value," "Top 15 in Sales," and "Top 15 in Profits" The Gap (fashion retailing) Homestake Mining (metals and mining) McKesson (pharmaceutical distribution) Pacific Gas and Electric (utility) Pacific Telesis Group (telephone) Potlatch (paper) Transamerica (financial services) Union Bank (bank) Wells Fargo (bank)

SAN MATEO COUNTY

Menlo Park Cisco Systems (computer software and services) Consolidated Freightways (trucking and shipping) Raychem (electrical products) *San Mateo* Franklin Resources (financial services) *South San Francisco* Genentech (drugs and research)

SANTA CLARA COUNTY

Cupertino Apple Computer (computers and peripherals) Measurex Corporation (electrical/ electronic instruments) Symantec (computer software and services) Tandem Computers (computers and peripherals) *Milpitas* LSI Logic (semiconduc-

tors) Quantum (computers and peripherals) *Mountain View* Acuson (medical products) Adobe Systems (computer software and services) Silicon Graphics (computers and peripherals) Software Publishing (computer software and services) Sun Microsystems (computers and peripherals) *Palo Alto* Alza (drugs and research) Hewlett-Packard Company (computers and peripherals) Syntex Corporation (drugs and research) Varian Associates (electronics) *San Jose* Cadence Design Systems (computer software and services) Conner Peripherals (computers and peripherals) Cypress Semiconductor (semiconductors) XILINX (semiconductors) *Santa Clara* Applied Materials (special machinery manufacturer) Intel Corporation (microprocessors)—world leader in microprocessor design and development National Semiconductor (semiconductors) Synoptics Communications (computer software and services) *Sunnyvale* Advanced Micro Devices (semiconductors) Amdahl Corporation (computers and peripherals) MIPS Computer Systems (computer software and services)

LEFT: Santa Clara County is home to the world-famous Silicon Valley. With about 3,000 high-tech companies, it is the region's economic power-house. Photo by Tom Tracy/The Photo File

▲ HIGH-TECH AND BIOTECH INDUSTRIES

"The importance of the high technology industries to the economic viability of the Bay Area cannot be overstated," according to Tapan Monroe, chief economist for Pacific Gas & Electric Company. Both high value-added manufacturing and service jobs are linked to these industries. Since 1960 high-tech manufacturing, particularly of electronics and computers, has emerged as the dominant manufacturing activity in the Bay Area.

Santa Clara County, home to Silicon Valley, stands on the leading edge of high technology with nearly 3,000 high-tech companies employing a quarter of a million people. Industries in Santa Clara County produce close to a quarter of the U.S. total output of computer storage devices, electron tubes, and semiconductors and related devices, making the county the leading manufacturer of those products. One of every three workers in the county is on a manufacturing payroll.

The Bay Area is also a leading center for the biotechnology and biosciences industries. Of the 200 biotech companies nationwide, about 35 percent are in California and more than 20 percent are in the Bay Area.

Emeryville, in Alameda County, is a focal point for what has become known as "Biotech Alley," or, as some others refer to it, "The Bionic Bay." Bioscience, or biotechnology, is barely 15 years old, but the Bay Area is preeminent as the industry's heartland. The University of California at Berkeley, the University's San Francisco Medical Center, and Stanford University are the nation's centers for bioscience research. Because of the proximity of these academic and medical resources, some of America's leading biotech companies have located in Emeryville, presenting the East Bay with the potential of being the national center of an emerging multibillion-dollar biotech industry. Bioscience is developing much like the computer industry, whose leap from the Stanford campus to Silicon Valley economically, scientifically and culturally transfused the area.

The PG&E plant in Martinez keeps residents comfortable in all types of weather. Photo by Bob Rowan/Progressive Image

Biotechnology industries are on the rise in the Bay Area, boasting more than 20 percent of the country's biotech companies. Alameda County leads the region in this emerging industry. Photo by Chris Springmann/The Photo File

PACIFIC GATEWAY

By Art Garcia

Since the 1970s each successive decade has been proclaimed by politicians, economists, government officials and trade experts as the beginning of the Pacific Era. The evidence is clear: the shift of the center of world economic activity from the Atlantic Ocean to the Pacific Ocean has begun, and the world is well on its way to what other prognosticators have predicted will be the Pacific Century.

Vital shipping networks in the air, on the ground, and at sea, all help to make the Bay Area a major economic center in both domestic and international markets. Photo by Robert Dawson/The Photo File

❏ ❏ ❏

International trade and investment plays a pivotal role in the Bay Area's economic community and Pacific Rim companies lead the way. Between 1984 and 1989, the Bay Area became the site for about 50 percent of all foreign-based Pacific-region businesses to locate in the United States. Photo by Mark E. Gibson

The nations on the western rim of the Pacific Basin—Japan, Korea, Taiwan, Hong Kong, Thailand, Malaysia, Singapore and the Philippines— have been the world's fastest-growing over the past three decades. America's own direction has followed this trend of prosperity by shifting toward the Pacific. And while most of the U.S. has posted rapid growth, no place has grown faster than California, the state that more than any other looks to Asia for trade, investment and immigration.

Though the Bay Area will grow more slowly than the rest of the state over the next 10 years, it can expect a population growth of about one million by the end of the decade and will post a faster growth rate than will the nation. Stephen Levy, director of the Center for the Continuing Study of the California Economy in Palo Alto, says the population surge is the result of national and global economic trends that should be particularly favorable to the economies of California and the Bay Area in the 1990s. He predicts international trade and investment, paced by the growth of the Pacific Basin, will play a greater role in the state and Bay Area economies. San Francisco is the vibrant hub of the Bay Area, the fourth-largest economic region in the U.S., with a gross regional product topping $140 billion. Estimates are that the regional economy is on track to become the third largest in the nation, further making the city's importance as an international business and financial center almost impossible to overstate.

▲ FOREIGN INVESTMENT

Pacific Rim investment in the Bay Area has increased steadily, and 49 of 106 foreign-owned Pacific-region companies established their U.S. headquarters in the Bay Area in the five years between 1984 and 1989, according to a 1990 survey by KPMG Peat Marwick, the international consulting and accounting firm. "It's no accident the level of foreign investment in the Bay Area is substantial and on the rise," says Jon Madonna, the firm's chairman. "After all," he adds, "we have outstanding port facilities, an excellent climate, access to major growth markets, and a host of support services for foreign-owned businesses, ranging from the consular corps and foreign chambers of commerce to international specialists among lawyers, accountants, tax consultants, bankers and other professional advisors."

KPMG Peat Marwick found that survey participants have invested more than $2.6 billion in property, plant and equipment as well as real estate in the Bay Area. Of companies surveyed, about 70 percent of total capital invested was by those representing Japan and Australia.

One of the world's model "factories of the future" had its origins in early 1982 when America's General Motors Corporation and Japan's Toyota Motor Corporation began discussing a possible joint venture operation in the U.S. A year later the two auto-manufacturing giants agreed to produce a subcompact car at the site of a former GM assembly plant in Fremont on the southeastern side of San Francisco Bay. The idea was to set up an independent company that would use production concepts and techniques similar to those used in Japan.

Named New United Motor Manufacturing, Inc., NUMMI for short, the joint company produced its first car, a Chevrolet Nova, in late 1984. Nova production continued until 1988. NUMMI turned out the Toyota Corolla FX from 1986 to 1988, and the plant now produces the

Geo Prizm for Chevrolet and the Toyota Corolla sedan for Toyota. In early 1991 expansion and modification of the plant was completed for production of a Toyota light-duty pickup truck, a $250-million project with an annual production rate of 100,000 units.

The NUMMI plant is located on 60 acres and has more than 3 million square feet of covered space. Total Bay Area employment of NUMMI, its suppliers, and contractors is 4,500 people and total investment in the venture has reached $750 million, with $200 million to be spent for truck production, bringing total investment to almost one billion dollars. Annual Bay Area payroll and purchases amount to $352 million. NUMMI's payroll of hourly and salaried employees numbers nearly 3,000, with an additional 800 workers hired last year for truck production. The Fremont facility has the capacity to produce about 220,000 passenger cars and 100,000 trucks a year.

Another Bay Area link to Asia is USS-POSCO Industries, California's largest steel producer and one of the world's most advanced steel-finishing

Pictured here is the production facility for New United Motor Manufacturing, Inc. This joint venture between America's General Motors Corporation and Japan's Toyota Motor Corporation was formed in 1982 and currently employs some 4,500 Bay Area workers, including suppliers and contractors. Photo by Gerald L. French/The Photo File

plants. An extensive $400-million modernization program transformed an 80-year-old steel-finishing mill at Pittsburg in east Contra Costa County (formerly owned and operated by U.S. Steel), into a state-of-the-art production facility for light, flat-rolled products. It was one of the largest investments in basic-manufacturing facilities ever made in Northern California.

USS-POSCO was set up in 1986 as an independent 50-50 joint venture between U.S. Steel Corporation, now known as USX, and Pohang Iron & Steel Company, Ltd. (POSCO) of the Republic of Korea, which claims to be the fastest-growing steel producer in the world. The company, one of the 10 largest private-sector employers in Contra Costa County, posts an annual payroll of $46 million and purchases more than $58 million a year in goods and services locally.

Along the Carquinez Strait, one of the oldest military arsenals in the West was declared surplus in the 1960s and sold to private interests, who, in turn, developed the property into an industrial park of more than 3,000 acres. Now operated as privately owned Benecia Industries, Inc., the Benicia property is an active maritime location for delivery of autos imported from Japan, Korea and Australia.

The Benecia general cargo terminal handles a substantial portion of autos for distribution from Northern California by rail-land-bridge shipment to other U.S. markets. Petroleum coke and asphalt crude also move through Northern California's largest port-oriented industrial park, a deep-water facility capable of berthing three vessels.

The Bay Area's political leadership is tuned in to the economic importance of international investment and trade and committed to encouraging their development. "The Bay Area also offers a unique advantage, in that Asian-Americans comprise almost one-quarter of the population," Jon Madonna notes, "and many maintain special cultural and economic ties with the Pacific Rim countries."

Strategically situated midway between Europe and Asia, the Bay Area is a natural center for trade and exports. The San Francisco Customs District alone handles nearly 40 percent of the state's export trade, which is valued at more than $16 billion. Photo by Chromosohm/Sohm

▲ EXPORTS

The region shares the state's role as the world's "one-stop shopping center," trading everything from agriculture, aerospace and autos to electronics, entertainment, and engines. To expand the exchange, California operates five trade and investment offices in Asia and Europe. The California Export Finance Office, with offices in San Francisco and Los Angeles, has supported nearly $200 million in export transactions.

The San Francisco Customs District handles 37 percent of California's export trade (valued at more than $16 billion) by sea and air. Nearly 50 countries maintain consulates and trade offices in San Francisco.

million people with an annual effective buying income of $130 billion. Backed also by a strong industrial-mineral base and a well-developed regional rail and highway transportation network leading from all parts of the continent, the Pacific Gateway swings wide for both exports and imports.

California sells 15 percent of all U.S. exports. At $63.1 billion, the state's 1991 exports continued to grow swiftly, reports the California World Trade Commission, although not at the same record-breaking pace of immediately prior years. The diverse industries of California and the Bay Area make both markets world suppliers.

Largest statewide exports in 1991 included

LEFT: Container ships such as this one have made the Port of Oakland one of the top 20 ports in the world in annual container traffic. Photo by Mark E. Gibson

FACING PAGE: Picturesque Carquinez Strait is a major Bay Area shipping route, handling cargo from automobiles to asphalt crude. Photo by Ed Cooper/The Photo File

Located midway between Europe and Asia, the Bay Area allows businesses to communicate with East and West global markets during the same day. Besides its trade activity with Southeast Asia, the Bay Area has major trading partners in Canada, Australia, New Zealand, Europe and Latin America. The European Economic Community, which will eliminate trade barriers among member countries by the end of 1992 and form a single market, will mean new trade opportunities.

The Bay Area's Pacific Gateway is hinged at the doorstep of California's richest agricultural regions and an expanding central state market of 7.5

general industrial machinery and computer equipment at $14.2 billion, electrical and electronic equipment of $13.1 billion, aerospace and transportation equipment valued at $10 billion, and foreign sales of food and crops that reached $6.1 billion. Total volume of goods passing in and out of California's harbors approaches $175 billion, creating jobs and nurturing the state's and the Bay Area's high quality of life. Foreign investment employs hundreds of thousands of Californians while pouring fresh capital and new technologies into an economy expected to become the world's fourth largest by the year 2000.

▲ WORLD TRADE CENTER

With its diversified and healthy economy, the Bay Area boasts one of the country's highest per capita income levels, a solid business growth rate, a rapidly increasing population, and a below-average unemployment rate.

Other important elements in the Bay Area's global growth include overseas air service from three Bay Area international airports plus deepwater ports in San Francisco, Oakland, Richmond and Redwood City.

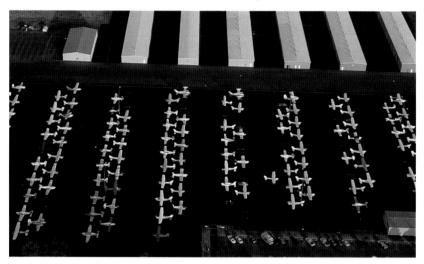

▲ AIR TRANSPORTATION

The Bay Area is the only region in the U.S. with three major international airports located within a few miles of each other. They include San Francisco, third busiest in the U.S. and eighth busiest in the world, Oakland, and San Jose. Barely 85 miles away is Sacramento Metropolitan Airport, which is served by seven national carriers and three commuter airlines. Concord's Buchanan Field across the Bay has scheduled commuter jet service to and from Southern California.

By the end of 1991, San Francisco International Airport, located 15 miles from downtown in San Mateo County, was the fifth-busiest U.S. airport in total passengers and third-largest origin and destination airport. More than 31.8 million travelers passed through its terminals, a daily average of nearly 87,000 passengers, and 418,638 landing and takeoff operations had been completed, 72 percent of them by commercial jet carriers.

SFO, as it's known in airline jargon, is a major world trade center for domestic and international traffic, serving overseas passengers as a gateway between the U.S. and the Pacific Basin. Seventy percent of all Bay Area air passengers in 1991

ABOVE: Concord's Buchanan Field has charter jet service to and from Southern California. Photo by Bob Rowan/ Progressive Image

RIGHT: A daily average of nearly 87,000 people pass through the terminals of San Francisco International. The airport is served by 55 airlines, providing flights to U.S. and international destinations. Photo by Tom Campbell/The Photo File

Completed in 1988 at a cost of $512 million, the modernization and renovation of San Francisco International Airport has resulted in a total of 80 gateways and 2.6 million square feet of terminal space. Photo by Tom Vano/The Photo File

BELOW: Bay Area Rapid Transit (BART) provides commuters with an alternative and efficient mode of transportation, serving the many diverse regions comprising the Bay Area. Photo by Chromosohm/ Sohm

moved through San Francisco International, a market share that held steady throughout the past decade.

The City of San Francisco owns SFO; and the airport, which supports itself, contributed $14 million to the City's general fund in fiscal 1992. The airport is served by 55 airlines providing direct service to more than 85 U.S. cities; 33 of those carriers provide service to more than 35 international destinations. Air-cargo volume in 1991 was 606,000 metric tons, ranking SFO sixth in U.S. air cargo tonnage. Plans are being completed for new cargo-handling facilities.

A $512-million modernization and renovation program was completed at SFO in 1988, giving the airport 80 aircraft gates, 48 of which can serve wide-body jets. Total terminal space comes to 2.6 million square feet. Since the international terminal opened in 1983, total foreign passenger traffic has increased 81 percent to 3.6 million yearly. That growth prompted SFO's master plan-

ners to call for construction of a new international terminal to handle the surge in traffic, especially from the Pacific.

The proposed terminal of 1.5 million square feet would have 22 gates for 747-400, four narrow-body gates, and a customs facility capable of processing 5,000 passengers hourly. Construction would include an automated people mover system to connect terminals with a new Ground Transportation Center and the long-term parking lot.

The system will be tied to BART, a direct airport connector line that will begin construction after politicians and local transportation agency officials settle a dispute over its location, and is part of BART's plans to extend its service down the peninsula. If approved, the new terminal would be completed by 1996 to handle expected air traffic growth of 10 percent annually through the year 2000.

Also in the plan is modernization of existing air-freight facilities, which, in 1989, handled more international cargo tonnage than domestic for the first time. SFO accounts for 97 percent of the Bay Area's international air-freight trade. In dollar volume this trade surpasses the combined total of all of the Bay Area's water ports by 16 percent.

A short hop across the Bay from SFO is Oakland International Airport, as is San Francisco Airport, also a bayside landfill facility. Operated by the Port of Oakland, the airport is within 40 minutes of 2.5 million Bay Area residents and is served by Interstate 80 and BART access. As aircraft and passenger volume increasingly crowd SFO, airlines and passengers are turning to the modern, but less busy, Oakland Airport. Located 10 miles from Oakland's downtown by car or BART, Oakland International serves 200 U.S. and foreign cities. Construction is underway to double the airport's capacity. Its North Field is the largest general aviation facility in the Bay Area.

Passenger activity at Oakland rose to 6.1 million in fiscal 1992 from the previous year's 6 million, while air-cargo traffic through the first 11 months of fiscal 1992 climbed to 531.1 million pounds from 431.4 million pounds. Major all-cargo carriers operating at Oakland include Airborne Freight, Burlington Air Express, Emery Worldwide, Federal Express, United Parcel Service, Ameriflight and Amerijet International.

United Airlines and Alaska Airlines have major maintenance facilities at Oakland International.

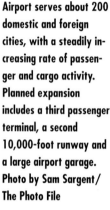

Oakland International Airport serves about 200 domestic and foreign cities, with a steadily increasing rate of passenger and cargo activity. Planned expansion includes a third passenger terminal, a second 10,000-foot runway and a large airport garage. Photo by Sam Sargent/ The Photo File

Southwest Airlines recently began operations at Oakland and quickly increased the airport's passenger traffic by 30 percent. United Airlines now has 20 flights daily out of Oakland.

Commercial aviation in San Jose made its debut in early 1949. Owned and operated by the City of San Jose, San Jose International Airport has kept pace with Santa Clara County and Silicon Valley through its $516-million Airport Development Program that includes three major new terminals

million passengers by the year 2006. With its recently opened new terminals, the airport becomes an even more critical link between the Bay Area and Southern California, the most heavily traveled air corridor in the world, and the South Bay, including Silicon Valley and the Monterey Peninsula.

Located two miles from downtown San Jose, the airport is served by more than 10 airlines that fly direct to more than 50 cities and provide

to carry the facility into the twenty-first century. San Jose, the county seat and one of the fastest-growing metropolitan areas in the U.S., became California's third-largest city and the nation's 12th-most populous in the late 1980s. By 1990 Santa Clara County, with a population of about 1.5 million, already was the largest California metropolitan area north of Los Angeles.

San Jose International, which in 1990 served six million passengers, is forecast to handle 18

connecting flights to worldwide destinations. It is second behind San Francisco International Airport in share of total Bay Area passenger volume. American Airlines in 1990 began transcontinental service out of San Jose and has made the airport its West Coast hub for expanded international service, beginning with nonstop service between San Jose and Tokyo. Flights originate and terminate in Boston, linking Silicon Valley businesses with high-tech centers in Japan and Boston.

Conveniently located just two miles from downtown San Jose, the San Jose International Airport is served by more than 10 carriers, including American Airlines. American has plans to make San Jose its West Coast hub for expanded international service. Photo by Gerald L. French/The Photo File

▲ The Ports

Airports of the Bay Area may log impressive growth statistics as they expand into the next decade, but most of their traffic gains are tied to a vital economy made healthy by international trade, and most of that passes through by ocean vessel.

World commerce is the cornerstone of California's powerful economy and the San Francisco Bay Area is a crossroads for trade routes and cultures that form America's gateway to the Pacific Basin—an aggregate market of $2.2 trillion and 1.6 billion potential consumers representing approximately a third of the world's total population. With one of the world's largest deep-water natural harbors, the Bay Area is where the Pacific Basin meets the United States, at the midpoint of America's western coast.

The ports of the Bay Area truly are the golden gateways for the trade gold rush of the second half of the twentieth century. Both the Port of San Francisco and Port of Oakland have carved out particular niches in serving the global marketplace by developing efficient handling of intermodal and container cargo.

Cargo king among Bay Area ports, which also include Redwood City, Richmond, inland to Sacramento and Stockton, as well as the privately operated Encinal Terminals in the Oakland Estuary and Port of Benecia in the Carquinez Strait, is the Port of Oakland. The third-largest port on the West Coast, it handles 16 percent of all containerized cargo primarily bound for Northern California, Southern Oregon and Western Nevada. Railroads distribute the bulk of the remaining container cargo, using double-stacked intermodal operations.

The Port of Oakland and Union Pacific Railroad have cooperated in a project to enlarge tunnels through the Sierra Nevada to allow double-stacked rail cars to pass and move even more cargo between Oakland and the rest of the U.S. Oakland's port also is the location of Jack London's Waterfront near downtown Oakland, a complex that is being revitalized with $100 million in new visitor and retail facilities, including hotels and restaurants.

With more than 550 acres of terminal facilities and 27 deep-water berths, the Port of Oakland is the largest on America's West Coast in physical size. It set the pace and paved the way for the intermodal container revolution and predictions

are that the port's container cargo volume will more than double over the decade of the 1990s. Projections state that by the twenty-first century's arrival the port will be pouring $8 billion a year into the Bay Area economy.

A current issue at the Port of Oakland is to win approval to dredge its inner and outer channels to 42 feet from 35 feet. Dredging is the Port of Oakland's highest priority and will enable it to more easily handle the generation of "post-Panamax" superships, so-called because they were built without regard to the limits imposed by the Panama Canal and designed especially to serve the lucrative Pacific trade routes between the U.S. and Asia.

When the dredging is completed, Oakland's container traffic should grow at a rate of 7 percent, ahead of the 5 percent rate for the rest of the West Coast. That would mean that by the year 2000, Oakland would be handling 26.7 million revenue tons annually, more than double the 14.5 million revenue tons of container cargo in

The Port of Oakland, the third-largest port on the West Coast, handles 16 percent of all containerized cargo primarily bound for Northern California, southern Oregon and western Nevada. Photo by Ed Gillmore/The Photo File

The Port of Oakland occupies 19 miles of waterfront on the eastern shore of San Francisco Bay and has more than 550 acres of terminal facilities. Photo by John Lund/The Photo File

1990. This activity generates nearly 30 percent of the City of Oakland's jobs, amounting to more than one billion dollars in yearly wages and salaries.

By the end of 1993, the port will have completed leasing of its $125-million Jack London's Waterfront development. The port has developed 462 acres of industrial land along its shoreline into restaurants, stores, shops and entertainment centers. Operating revenues from the port's commercial real estate in fiscal 1992 came to $8.2 million.

The Port of Oakland was the first West Coast port to invest heavily in container handling. It occupies 19 miles of waterfront on the eastern or mainland shore of San Francisco Bay and has more than 550 acres of terminal facilities, 28 deep-water berths, including 19 that serve container, combination container/breakbulk, and roll-on/roll-off ships, plus 25 container cranes. Containers generate most of the port's revenues, but they aren't the only cargo traffic moving through Oakland. The port has an array of specialized facilities to handle break-bulk (or non-containerized) imports and exports, including steel, autos, and heavy equipment.

Since the first containership berthed at Oakland in 1962, the port has blossomed into one of the largest container port on the North American Pacific Coast, and it ranks among the top 20 ports in the world in annual container traffic. Four major

routes serve the port: the Union Pacific and Southern Pacific/Denver & Rio Grande Western routes through the Central Gateway and the Southern Pacific and Santa Fe routes through the Southwest.

Oakland, without question, has been the dominant Bay Area port, overshadowing the Port of San Francisco in oceangoing commerce. But the once-slumbering Port of San Francisco awakened in the 1980s with a new vitality, a new strategy and a new outlook. Since cargo ships have gotten bigger and gone intermodal, San Francisco decided to promote the advantages of its 42-foot natural deep-water side of the bay. Until Oakland completes its dredging, many ships will have to continue sailing or arriving there at high tide. Besides deep-water access, the Port of San Francisco also has direct rail service from its piers.

Major waterfront revitalization projects are underway on port property along the 7.5 miles and 850 acres of San Francisco's Embarcadero. Pier 39, an entertainment complex of shops and restaurants, and Fisherman's Wharf are among San Francisco's most popular tourist attractions. In fiscal 1991 the port had operating revenues of $33.1 million. About half the operating revenues came from property and commercial ventures, while maritime operations accounted for 35 percent. Total tonnage, including containers, breakbulk and bulk cargo, was more than

3.1 million tons. San Francisco, meanwhile, remained the premiere coffee port of the western U.S.

On the passenger cruise side of the port's maritime business, San Francisco's Port Commission unanimously accepted a proposal for building an international cruise terminal at South Beach, near the Bay Bridge. The commission has received a plan by a Danish investor group to finance a $130-million Scandinavia Center cruise terminal complex that would include two ship berths, a 360-room hotel and conference center, restaurants, shops, and offices.

In early 1990 the Port Commission approved a long-awaited strategic plan that puts major decisions on port land use into a larger framework. Earlier approval of a waterfront hotel was criticized, partly because it had no larger context.

The plan highlights land-use and development issues with full public participation in development decisions. It also calls for improved container-handling facilities, support for commercial fishing, better customer service, and tighter fiscal management. San Francisco voters in the November 1990 general election, however, approved a city measure that limits hotels on port property and calls for the creation of a master land-use plan.

Of the smaller Bay Area ports, Richmond primarily handles liquid petroleum and chemicals for processors and Redwood City handles dry bulk, such as salt from nearby solar evaporation operations. The ports of Stockton and Sacramento are more than 50 miles upriver from the Bay and principally handle grain and other dry products that arrive on standard ocean carriers.

Since the first container ships berthed at Oakland in 1962, the port has blossomed into one of the largest container ports on the North American Pacific coast. Photo by Kerrick James

▲ GROUND TRANSPORTATION

Interstate highways and transcontinental railways meet and crisscross the Bay Area, creating an inter-modal air-sea-land gateway to California and the West and to America's vast market east of the Sierra Nevada.

The railroads that opened the American West today serve as a vital connector in the import-export trade for the nation, California and the Bay Area. The City and Port of San Francisco are served by the Southern Pacific, Union Pacific and Atchison, Topeka & Santa Fe railroads. Southern Pacific has direct trackage to the Peninsula, while the other lines offer normal drayage to railhead services.

number of industrial parks, mining, timber and agricultural land properties, as well as Southern Pacific's former petroleum products and pipeline-leasing subsidiaries. Not included, however, was Southern Pacific Transportation Company, the rail-road part of the business and several small trucking subsidiaries.

The Interstate Commerce Commission consid-ered a merger of Southern Pacific and Santa Fe railroads in a long, drawn-out case, then finally de-cided the merger would be non-competitive, rejected it and ordered Santa Fe Southern Pacific to divest one of the two railroads. As a result, Southern Pacific Transportation was sold to Rio

RIGHT: Recent Bay Area rail activity is putting Santa Clara County on track to becoming an im-portant rail center as well as strengthening the re-gion's role as a Pacific Rim trade hub. Photo by Chromosohm/Sohm

FACING PAGE: The San Francisco railroads serve as a vital connection for the import/export business throughout the Bay Area, California, and the nation. Photo by Chromosohm/Sohm

San Francisco-based Southern Pacific Company, a major factor in western and Bay Area history, has diversified well beyond the railroad. It started truck lines in the 1920s, became a major landholder, and in 1969 reorganized into a holding company, plac-ing its railroad and trucking operations under the subsidiary called Southern Pacific Transportation Company.

In late 1983 the holding company merged with Santa Fe Industries to form what is now Santa Fe Southern Pacific Corporation. Included in the merger were Southern Pacific land holdings, including development projects such as Mission Bay along San Francisco's southern waterfront, a

Grande Industries, which also owns the Denver & Rio Grande Western Railroad.

The combined 15,000-mile, 15-state system, the nation's fifth-largest rail network, operates with separate identities (but under the Southern Pacific banner) from San Francisco headquarters. It offers direct access to most West Coast and Gulf Coast ports and most Mexican and eastern gateways.

More than half of today's West Coast cargo pool is destined for or originates from the larger markets east of the Rockies. The merger of South-ern Pacific with the Denver & Rio Grande created a unified and competitive rail system linking Northern California, the strongest export-oriented

ABOVE: By the year 2000 CalTrain service between San Francisco and San Jose is projected to move more than 100 trains a day, extending as far south as Monterey. Photo by Kerrick James

RIGHT: Some 1,500 trucking companies serve the shipping needs of the Bay Area's nine counties. Photo by Sam Sargent/ The Photo File

economy and home to the fourth-largest metropolitan market in the country, to the vital Midwest "bread basket."

The Port of San Francisco, which built California's first on-dock intermodal container transfer facility in 1986, is concluding negotiations with Southern Pacific to modify two old rail tunnels in San Francisco for clearance of double-stack high cube containers. When construction is completed, the multimillion-dollar capital improvement project will provide unrestricted cargo access, from ship direct to rail and straight from the port on a single-line haul through America's central rail corridor. Completion of one of the last pieces needed in the port's modern intermodal infrastructure will provide a "level playing field" for competition against Pacific Northwest and Southern California ports for the burgeoning intermodal market.

Four major rail routes serve the Port of Oakland: the Union Pacific and the Southern Pacific/Denver & Rio Grande Western routes through the Central Gateway and the Southern Pacific and Santa Fe routes through the Southwest. Clearance for double-stack container unit trains is available over the Union Pacific Central Gateway route through the Sierra Nevada mountains, as well as via the Southern Pacific route to the Southwest.

Meanwhile, recent Bay Area rail activity is putting Santa Clara County on track to become an important rail center and further strengthen the region's role as a Pacific Rim trade hub. Within several years, with $85 million funded from passage of a California ballot measure in June 1990, four Amtrak passenger trains will complete daily runs each way between San Jose and Auburn in the Sierra foothills east of Sacramento, making 19 stops along the way.

Plans call for 10 daily trains in each direction to ease traffic on Interstate 80, one of Northern California's busiest freeways. About 6,000 passengers are expected to make the daily run initially, but by the end of the century that number could rise to 22,000. Projections are that these services will more closely tie the economies of Santa Clara and Sacramento counties in time.

With voter approval of transportation bond measures, CalTrain service between San Francisco and San Jose and southern points is being expanded. By the year 2000 that corridor is projected to

Multilane freeways and interstates provide a vital link in the region's transportation network. Photo by Pete Saloutos/ The Photo File

move more than 100 trains a day, extending as far south as Monterey. CalTrain's estimates are that train service would accommodate between 80,000 and 100,000 riders a day, compared with 22,000 at the end of 1990.

On still another rail front effecting Santa Clara County, Southern Pacific Transportation Company and a tri-county group, the Joint Powers Board, are nearing agreement for the railroad to sell 120 miles of track for a price ranging between $150 million and $300 million. Under this plan, Southern Pacific would sell several spurs and branch lines between San Francisco and San Jose to the JPB, with SP and the Port of San Francisco retaining freight access. The three counties—San Francisco, San Mateo and Santa Clara—would use the acquired track as part of their mass transit operations. Port and Southern Pacific officials hope to see freight service expanded in the near future. Work is scheduled to get underway by July 1993 on an $11-million project to bring double-stack rail service into San Francisco by September 1994 through two existing tunnels.

The largest other land freight-shipping company based in the Bay Area is Consolidated Freightways, Inc., a diversified transportation concern headquartered in Menlo Park. Its main businesses are in long-haul and regional trucking throughout North America, domestic and international air freight, and intermodal rail and ocean freight services. Consolidated Freightways, which celebrated its 60th anniversary in 1989, also is involved in air freight charters, customs brokerage, and warehousing. During the past decade, CF's annual revenues increased fourfold, from just less than one billion dollars to more than $4 billion.

Consolidated Freightways Corporation, more commonly known as CF Motor Freight, is the company's largest and oldest subsidiary. Emery Worldwide, another subsidiary, is an integrated air-freight carrier that provides overnight door-to-door delivery of air cargo throughout North America and to 90 countries via a fleet of 80 aircraft.

Overall, motor freight services are extensive, with about 1,500 trucking firms and 30,000 employees in the Bay Area's nine counties. Shipping in the region has become more decentralized as the regional economy evolves from manufacturing to service, retail, and other people-intensive industries. Modern, multilane freeways and interstate highways will be extended, thanks to California voter approval in June 1990 of three ballot propositions that will not only fund transportation projects through bond issues, but also raise the gas tax to pay for upkeep and expansion.

Postcard views of San Francisco mostly focus on the Golden Gate Bridge as a Bay Area symbol, but the Bay Bridge between that city and Oakland is the region's busiest cross-water artery. The daily vehicle count is about 250,000 traveling east and west over the bridge. Although important to regional transportation, the Bay Bridge is only a spoke in the area's well-developed transportation wheel.

When the October 1989 Loma Prieta earthquake caused a section of the bridge to collapse, closing the Bay Bridge to traffic for a month, regional transportation agencies coordinated use of the Golden Gate, San Mateo, Dumbarton, Richmond, Carquinez, and Benicia bridges with cross-bay ferries and the Bay Area Rapid Transit District (BART) to keep people, goods, and the local economy moving. "The earthquake showed the strength of the Bay Area's transportation infrastructure, a present and growing asset," the San Francisco Chamber of Commerce concluded in its 1990 Bay Area Business Report.

As twilight settles over the Bay Area, San Francisco's renowned fog rolls past the landmark Golden Gate Bridge and into the bay. Photo by Gerald L. French/The Photo File

NETWORKS

 aintaining a dynamic and consistent flow of power, people, and data both inside and outside the Bay Area is the responsibility of energy, transportation, and communication suppliers.

▲ KKSF-FM (103.7) ▲ GTEL

▲ Pacific Gas and Electric

▲ KKHI-AM (1550) and FM (95.7)

▲ San Francisco Business Times

▲ KCBS Newsradio (74)

Photo by Chromosohm/Sohm

❏ ❏ ❏

KKSF-FM (103.7)

K KSF, 103.7 FM, is that rare Bay Area radio station that talks softly and carries a big audience.

Mixing adult contemporary, soft rock, contemporary jazz, and New Age music—much of it uncharted by the radio and record industries—KKSF produces a sound that is both soothing and stimulating, programming that flows evenly, with minimal interruptions. Its announcers never talk over songs, and the title and artist of each selection are announced after every set of songs. The station also maintains, through its programming and sponsorships, a strong commitment to public service.

KKSF calls it "Music Without Borders." Industry observers call it "new adult contemporary." Whatever its format label, KKSF consistently ranks among the top five stations in San Francisco in attracting upscale listeners, ages 25 to 54.

Attracting this choice demographic group has taken exhaustive research and not a little daring. When Brown Broadcasting Company bought the station in the spring of 1987 it featured traditional adult-contemporary programming and ranked 33rd in the market in the 25-to-54 age group. In an effort to boost its ratings, the station's new management considered other, traditional forms of niche programming—adult

contemporary, country, and album rock—before the decision was made to venture onto new turf.

Launching a format that had been used with limited success only a couple times before in other parts of the country, KKSF focused on jazz fusion, New Age music, and vocalists who wouldn't otherwise get exposure on radio. The ratings quickly improved. The KKSF style, in which announcers shun "radio personality" hype for an intelligent yet low-key delivery and emphasis on music, was catching on.

The station's climb, adds KKSF general manager David Kendrick, has been enhanced by the unconventional nature of the Bay Area market. "It's a progressive market," says Kendrick, noting that San Francisco, home of KKSF studios, has a history of introducing new formats, such as album-oriented rock, to the nation's airwaves. "This area allows a tremendous amount of flexibility in terms of lifestyle, in terms of acceptance of things that are new and different."

KKSF is indeed new and different, even considering the variety of programming offered by the more than 70 radio signals competing for listener attention in the Bay Area. More important, KKSF has capitalized on its uniqueness. Absent are screaming disc jockeys, hokey promotions, gimmicks, and schmaltz. KKSF's mission is to offer respite from noisy extremes, to soothe daily stresses with knowledgeable presentations and music programming that can be listened to throughout the day.

One of the target markets in KKSF's broad-based audience is, in fact, office listeners. The weekday musical blend, for example, is designed

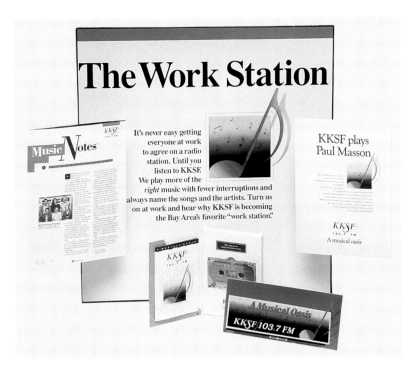

KKSF's advertising and promotion is as unique as its format. Shown are examples of KKSF's targeted direct mail, transit, magazine ads, billboards, and listener newsletters.

to complement the moods and activities associated with each segment of the workday: an energetic mix for morning and afternoon commutes, and a calmer mix favoring instrumentals during midday office hours. Instrumental pieces also are favored in the evenings, establishing a tranquil mood to help listeners unwind.

Spyro Gyra, Sade, Pat Metheny, the Gypsy Kings, Bonnie Raitt, David Sanborn, instrumentalists on the Windham Hill label—KKSF draws on these and dozens of other local and internationally known artists in shaping its sound. The station also has a long and growing list of artists, including Kenny G, Bobby McFerrin, and Acoustic Alchemy, who have performed live over the air from KKSF studios. Naturally, when these musicians give concerts in the Bay Area, KKSF is one of their principal sponsors.

But there is more to KKSF than meets the ear. Its thoughtful approach to radio and respectful treatment of listeners go hand-in-hand with the station's public-service orientation. One popular KKSF amenity is the BayLine©, an internally programmed phone service that provides traffic, news, weather, and music, including the latest additions to the KKSF playlist and the names of record retailers who carry the music.

The station further strengthens its relationship with listeners through outside events such as Listener Parties, which feature live music by artists heard on KKSF (one recent party drew more than 5,000 people), and through MusicNotes©, KKSF's quarterly newsletter and listener guide. MusicNotes© is sent to the entire KKSF database and features the playlist, concert calenders, artist interviews, and more.

By far the station staff's proudest achievement, however, has been its fundraising success for the San Francisco AIDS Foundation, a pioneer organization in AIDS education and advocacy. Forming its own in-house record company, the station put together the KKSF AIDS Relief Sampler, an album of songs donated by 14 of KKSF's most popular artists, including Basia, Larry Carlton, and Kenny G.

Released in the fall of 1989, Sampler 1 has sold over 40,000 copies and KKSF has presented proceeds totalling over $150,000. Sampler 2, released in July of 1991, has also sold in excess of 40,000 copies and raised over $250,000. These sums represent the largest corporate donation in the history of the San Francisco AIDS Foundation and underscore music's power to heal as well as entertain. Sampler 3 is due to be released in the fall of 1992.

LEFT: The healing power of music: Sales of KKSF Samplers 1 and 2 have raised more than $400,000 for the San Francisco AIDS Foundation.

GTEL

In the early 1980s the Federal Communications Commission and the California Public Utilities Commission delivered a one-two blow to the comfortable status quo of the telecommunications business:

• The FCC ordered a historic split between the telecommunications equipment business and the telecommunications service business; the marketing of equipment was deregulated and thrown open to competition, while transmission service providers continued under regulated, government-granted monopolies.

• The California PUC followed up the FCC order by telling GTE California—which was in both businesses—that if it wished to remain a marketer of equipment, it would have to form a completely separate subsidiary to do it.

GTE California had no intention of abandoning the customers who for decades had depended on the company for all their telecommunications needs. It accepted the challenge of creating a subsidiary with the creativity, aggressiveness, and quick reflexes demanded by a wide open market—and in 1985 GTE California launched GTEL, a wholly owned subsidiary.

GTEL was a curious mix of regal corporate pedigree and venture capitalist feistiness, and still is. The customer premises equipment (CPE) market is the telephone business' Bermuda Triangle—a lot of companies enter it and disappear. But seven years afters its inception, GTEL is not only surviving, but prospering.

The secret of GTEL's success is that it refuses to be intimidated by anything. It has consistently tackled projects that seemed too big and ideas that seemed too new. And flying in the face of conventional wisdom has paid off handsomely.

The most illustrative and dramatic example of this trait is the vast telecommunications network GTEL is building for the state of California—CALNET. The only American public institution larger than the state government of California is the federal government, and the state's telecommunications and information management needs were commensurate with the scope of its operations.

GTEL, as usual, was unruffled by the challenge. It conceived a statewide network that would vastly upgrade quality and the range of available services, and save money while it was doing it. It put together an all-star team of subcontractors—IBM, MCI, Northern Telecom, and GTE Telecomm. It staged a spectacular, real-life demonstration of CALNET's potential that impressed state experts. And it faced down the competition, including a court challenge.

The result is a state-of-the-art, cost-effective new network for the state of California and another improbable but undeniable win for GTEL.

And CALNET is merely one very visible example of a long list of high-wire walks, including:

CALNET—California's communication network for 1992 and beyond.

• Reinventing the concept of the GTE Phone Mart—GTE's national, 120-location retail chain for CPE—by creating the "Multi-Mart," an innovative approach to serving both residential and small-business customers in the same store.

• Leading the rest of the telecommunications industry into the "electronic funds transfer" business—ATMs. ATMs were generally regarded as a financial business until GTEL planners took a second look and saw that they were computers wired to data bases and to each other. That, they realized, is a telecommunications business, and GTEL leaped in.

However, at GTEL, feats of entrepreneurship don't overshadow a more venerable GTE value: a fierce commitment to customer service. While GTEL's sales force is confounding the competition, its highly trained, highly experienced technicians—with an average tenure in the business of 15 years—are making sure that everything works as promised.

An uneasy combination of gleeful adventurousness and salt-of-the-earth conservatism? Absolutely. GTEL wouldn't have it any other way.

And neither would seven years' worth of satisfied customers.

ABOVE AND LEFT: GTEL has continually embraced the newest technologies and the biggest projects. The company has provided products and services for the county of Sacramento and the U.C. Davis Medical Center.

PACIFIC GAS AND ELECTRIC

Pacific Gas and Electric Company, a California institution founded in 1905, is proving that a company in a mature business can be an innovative force in meeting changing customer and community needs.

PG&E's service territory—94,000 square miles in northern and central California—includes 48 of the state's 58 counties, with a population of more than 11.8 million. Standing alone, PG&E's territory would be the 12th largest economy in the world. The diversified market the company serves includes high-tech electronics, agriculture, food processing, petroleum refining, aerospace manufacturing, tourism, transportation, financial services, and wood products.

PG&E's electric business annually provides customers with more than 90 million killowatt-hours of power. The company generates and purchases electricity generated by a wide range of resources: hydro, geothermal, nuclear, natural gas, biomass, solar, and wind.

PG&E's natural gas business serves more than 3 million residential customers, 200,000 commercial customers, and 2,000 industrial users. In recent years the company has acquired approximately half its gas from California and the American Southwest, and the other half from Canada.

Looking to the future, PG&E has developed an innovative approach toward addressing a key challenge: meeting growing customer demands for energy while safeguarding the environment.

The heart of this strategy is the company's

"green" electric resource plan. PG&E plans to meet 75 percent of its peak electric demand growth during the 1990s through customer energy efficiency—a smarter use of energy employing new technologies to control costs without sacrificing comfort, convenience, or productivity. As part of the plan, rebates are being given to residential, commercial, industrial, and agricultural customers for installing energy-efficient equipment.

The company is working with the Natural Resources Defense Council, Rocky Mountain Institute, and Lawrence Berkeley Laboratory to test new ways to increase energy efficiency. It also operates the Pacific Energy Center in San Francisco to demonstrate cost-effective and energy-efficient lighting systems and construction technologies.

PG&E also plans to continue meeting customers' electricity needs through a clean resource mix. The company is active in realizing the full potential of renewable resources, and is a national leader in promoting the development of wind and solar energy for large-scale utility use.

PG&E has a wide range of environmental programs, with a professional staff responsible for monitoring and protecting land, air, water, and wildlife. PG&E has received numerous honors for its environmental programs, including the first-ever Pollution Reduction Award from the California Air Resources Board for reducing hydrogen sulfide emissions at its geothermal plants by 90 percent, while also reducing hazardous wastes by 80 percent.

Concern for the environment by PG&E's customers, shareholders, and employees has led the company to new business ventures. The company's Clean Air Vehicle program promotes the use of clean-burning natural gas for fleet vehicles and supports the development of electric cars.

PG&E recognizes that its success as a company is dependent upon the well-being of the people it serves, and so with the help of its 26,000 employees, it plays an active role in maintaining the vitality of communities. The company serves a wide range of human service, educational, environmental, civic, and cultural organizations. In 1991, philanthropic contributions totaled $6 million.

Education is a special concern of the company. PG&E works with many community groups to develop strategies and coalitions to improve

Energy-efficient lighting is just one of the many technologies PG&E promotes through its Customer Energy Efficiency Programs.

The two units of the Diablo Canyon Nuclear Power Plant in San Luis Obispo County produce about 20 percent of the electricity generated by PG&E.

local educational systems. The company is especially interested in math and science education, and in addressing the needs of youth at risk.

The company's grants also focus on employment and economic self-sufficiency. In addition, the Community Service Awards Program distributes grants to organizations with PG&E volunteers. But the company endeavors to assist people meet whatever challenges come their way—as with the 1989 Loma Prieta earthquake. For its safe and rapid restoration of vital energy services following that disaster, PG&E received the Edison Award from the Edison Electric Institute, an award honoring the company that best serves as a role model for other utilities.

The increased deregulation of utilities, and the subsequent rise of competition, poses a challenge to PG&E, but also presents opportunities. In 1988 the company formed a subsidiary,

PG&E Enterprises, in order to apply its knowledge and experience to new business ventures from coast to coast.

Enterprises runs four businesses: U.S. Generating Company, in Bethesda, Maryland, develops, manages, and owns independent power plants; U.S. Operating Services, also in Maryland, supplies operating and maintenance services to U.S. Generating Company projects; PG&E Resources, located in Dallas, Texas, acquires, explores for, develops, and produces natural gas and oil resources; and PG&E Properties, based in Concord, California, develops property in PG&E's service territory.

PG&E's vigorous approach toward meeting today's challenges and preparing for tomorrow's opportunities promise a bright future—for the company, its customers, its shareholders, and the communities it serves.

KKHI-AM (1550) AND FM (95.7)

Classical-music station KKHI reaches its audience in ways as varied—and rewarding—as the classical repertoire itself.

Simulcast 24 hours a day on AM (1550) and FM (95.7), KKHI's signal extends from Sacramento to the Santa Cruz mountain range, a geographic area that includes two of the nation's largest classical markets: San Francisco and San Jose.

Shunning "stuffed-shirt classical" pretension, the station appeals to all types of classical listeners, from neophytes to longtime devotees. And KKHI's knowledgeable announcers take obvious pleasure in presenting selections from the more than 20,000 compact discs in KKHI's classical library, one of the country's largest.

This foundation of recorded fare is augmented by a wide variety of live and tape-delayed broadcasts. KKHI is, for example, the radio voice of the San Francisco Symphony, San Francisco Opera, San Francisco Ballet, the Marin Symphony, and three other regional symphony orchestras. The Metropolitan Opera, Cleveland Orchestra, Chicago Orchestra, St. Louis Symphony, and others also highlight the weekly broadcast schedule.

Owned since 1964 by Buckley Broadcasting Corporation of Greenwich, Connecticut, KKHI occupies one of the most demographically desirable niches in the Bay Area radio market, catering largely to affluent, well-educated professionals and managers 35 and older. At the same time, the station is continually bringing younger listeners into the classical music fold—those who will account for the largest

group of potential KKHI listeners 10 and 15 years into the future.

"We've been striving for a more youthful sound on the station," says general manager Bruce Beebe, adding that KKHI takes special pride in cosponsoring the annual San Francisco Symphony Young Musicians Awards competitions, which showcase the musical talents of high school and college students throughout the Bay Area.

Operating from the 14th floor of the St. Francis Hotel, in the heart of San Francisco's Union Square shopping district, KKHI broadcasts its AM signal in stereo, while its FM signal is enhanced by an electronic technology called FMX. But many of its listeners think of KKHI as much for its community outreach services as for its high-quality radio product.

The station sponsors two toll-free telephone services, one providing daily updates on classical music events, the other, called the CD Information Line, dispensing information, and even advice, about classical CD recordings. Also free for the asking is "Listener Guild," a quarterly KKHI newsletter that includes profiles of on-air personalities and reminders about special broadcasts and upcoming community events.

In many cases, KKHI is principal sponsor and promoter of these events, whether they be private art showings or summertime classical music concerts at Concord Pavilion in Concord. It's all toward KKHI's overall objective, says general manager Beebe: "We want not only to be with you while you're driving to work or at the office, but to be a little bit more of a way of life for our listeners—a good, constant companion."

SAN FRANCISCO BUSINESS TIMES

San Francisco Business Times readers are at the core of Bay Area business activity. A 1991 survey shows that 72 percent of the newspaper's 11,000 subscribers are top executives in their businesses and that 54 percent are owners or partners. These readers are important decision makers in Bay Area business, and the San Francisco Business Times helps them make sound decisions.

Part of a nationwide chain of 26 business journals owned by Charlotte, North Carolina–based American City Business Journals Inc., the weekly paper has been serving the Bay Area since September 1986. Its editorial staff, which is constantly in touch with the events, people, and political dynamics affecting Bay Area businesses, provides readers with consistent, compelling coverage. Just as important, the San Francisco Business Times goes beyond breaking news, analyses, and commentary to foreshadow national and regional trends.

It is also a visually handsome paper, with a crisp tabloid layout and clearly presented graphics and design elements that in 1990 earned it the "best overall design" award in a national competition conducted by Association of Area Business Publications (AABP). AABP judges were particularly impressed with the San Francisco Business Times' easy-to-read format.

Other regular San Francisco Business Times features include the Top 25 list of firms and business leaders; "People on the Move," which charts personnel changes; and "On File," a listing of new businesses and other business information not published elsewhere. The newspaper also produces several supplemental publications throughout the year, including the Small Business Resource Guide, The "How To" book, a pratical buying guide for growing companies, and the annual Book of Lists, an updated compilation of the year's Top 25 lists that has become the single most popular Business Times product.

The continuing editorial emphasis, however, is on the news and analysis offered in the main news section each week, coverage that continues to earn the newspaper its status as a "must read" publication.

The San Francisco Business Times has a total circulation of 14,000, with approximately 11,000 paid subscribers and 4,000 to 5,000 copies mailed each week to a highly qualified sample group as part of an ongoing subscription conversion campaign. Marketing research conducted in 1991 shows there are 2.6 readers per copy, for a total readership of 41,000.

The Newspaper currently is expanding its coverage and circulation in the East Bay counties of Alameda and Contra Costa and in San Mateo and Marin counties. According to publisher Mary Huss, "It is our intention to be the authority on business throughout the Bay Area, and to provide businesses with thorough, useful, high impact information on local business they won't find anywhere else."

Regarding future growth of the newspaper, Huss says, "Our most important investment is in the depth, quality, and continued high journalistic standards of our editorial product and in the training and development of our editing and reporting team."

San Francisco Business Times Publications.

KCBS NEWSRADIO (74)

K CBS provides something Bay Area residents need but don't have time to wait in line for: news. Broadcasting 24 hours a day at 740 on the AM dial, KCBS Newsradio instantly connects its listeners to the world outside their home, car, or office.

With traffic and weather updates every 10 minutes, business and sports every half hour, and a constant flow of local and world news, KCBS listeners get the information they need quickly and accurately, and then move on to other activities—even other radio stations.

Which is exactly as KCBS intends it.

Recognizing the diversity of the Bay Area radio market, KCBS doesn't attempt to be its listeners' "one and only" station, just their favorite news station. Rather than target a narrow demographic group, KCBS presents itself to a broad, sophisticated audience as one element in a radio diet that also very likely includes a music station, a sports station, a talk-show program, or any of a variety of other formats.

"We're dealing with people whose lives have become more full," says KCBS general manager and vice president Frank Oxarart. "You have to figure out how you fit into their lives."

For KCBS, fitting into listeners' busy schedules means distilling the vast amounts of material that comprise modern radio news— everything from the time to traffic to breaking local news to international affairs—into a potent and concise product. It is a technique KCBS has mastered.

The station's success in news programming,

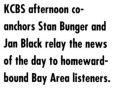

in fact, has won it more broadcasting awards than any other Bay Area radio station.

An important part of KCBS' news coverage, especially of national and international stories, comes from the vast news network and affiliates of CBS, Inc., which has owned KCBS since 1949. But the station's journalistic forte is its live coverage of events in the greater Bay Area, coverage supplied by reporters operating out of

KCBS' Embarcadero Center offices in San Francisco and bureaus in Alameda, Contra Costa, Sacramento, and Santa Clara counties.

This approach to regional news, notes Oxarart, has been evolving since 1968, when KCBS shifted from a full-service format, which included entertainment programming, to an all-news format.

To say the least, all-news radio has dramatically improved since the late sixties. In its original incarnation, this format included a lot of "rip and read" items—news stories culled directly from newspaper clips and wire-service copy.

In its current form, KCBS' all-news radio is a showcase for the best in timely, live coverage, which is enhanced by the reporting staff's knowledge of the communities

the Loma Prieta earthquake in 1989 and the Persian Gulf War in 1991 would severely test the mettle and skills of any news organization, KCBS has proven itself to be at the top of its field in meeting such challenges. Its coverage of the earthquake, for example, earned KCBS the prestigious George Foster Peabody, Sigma Delta Chi, and Alfred I. du Pont awards for outstanding work. Just as significant, the station regularly wins international, national, and regional awards—there were 29 of them in 1990—for its day-to-day programming.

KCBS also occupies a place of honor in radio history as the first station in the United States to produce regular broadcasts. Originally located in San Jose, the station came on the air against a backdrop of emerging turn-of-the-century tech-

KCBS newsroom editors and writers constantly gather and check information, ensuring accurate, up-to-date news reports.

throughout the KCBS broadcast area. And it is a huge area. Attracting most of its listeners from the 35-plus age group, the station reaches north-to-south from Chico to Bakersfield, and east-to-west from the Sierra Nevada to the Pacific Ocean.

Maintaining a news operation of this scale is expensive, Oxarart admits, but essential to effective regional coverage. "We started our own news-gathering to try to make sense of what was going on in the region," he says, adding, "I don't know how much impact we have when KCBS talks about what Congress is doing, but we can certainly have a strong impact when we talk about what the state legislature is doing and what the city government is doing."

While the quicksilver nature of events such as

nology: Italian inventor Guglielmo Marconi patented his wireless telegraph in 1897; in 1903 Canadian Reginald Fessenden had sent wireless voice messages using an arc transmitter; and in 1910 Californian Lee de Forest used his invention of the three-element electron tube to transmit as well as receive radio waves.

But it seemed to Charles David Herrold, a San Jose resident who had studied engineering at Stanford University, that radio had a future beyond two-way wireless communication, the main focus of radio experiments at the time. In 1909 Herrold opened the Herrold College of Engineering and, using a 15-watt transmitter built atop the Garden City Bank Building in San Jose, began the nation's first daily broadcasts.

Programming was not yet a science, of

RIGHT: KCBS news and program director Ed Cavagnaro, shown here discussing coverage of a breaking story with the editorial staff.

BELOW: KCBS afternoon traffic reporter George Rask provides commuter traffic information to KCBS listeners.

course. Herrold and assistant Ray Newby played music, read the news and offered commentary on it, and identified the station with "This is San Jose calling." At Herrold's urging, his wife Sybil became radio's first woman disc jockey, playing records provided in a trade-out with a local music store. Herrold also found himself supplying receiver sets to area residents interested in listening to the station's broadcasts.

Shut down by the government during World War I, the station was later reactivated and in 1921 was licensed and assigned the call letters KQW. (KDKA, in Pittsburgh, Pennsylvania, received the country's first broadcast license and call letters in 1920.) In 1925 Herrold sold the station to the First Baptist Church in San Jose, which interpolated KQW as "the King's Quickening Word." The station passed through two more owners before CBS purchased it in 1949 and renamed it KCBS.

Although Herrold's engineering school was the only business initially promoted by the station, Herrold and his successors at KQW soon found themselves at the forefront in exploring radio's commercial possibilities. KQW's first advertiser was the Sperry Flour Company, which in 1926 bought time on a daily cooking program. Herrold himself went on to become an advertising consultant for several radio stations.

In 1942 the station moved its studios from San Jose to San Francisco's Palace Hotel, the same year it established, as an affiliate, its first business ties with CBS. Proclaiming itself "the stars' address," KCBS became a showcase for some of the best radio programming of the forties and fifties, including live music (the station had two orchestras on staff), live studio audiences, and variety-show fare that attracted top entertainers and a huge share of the greater Bay Area's radio audience.

In spite of past successes, however, KCBS never lost its knack for innovation. In the early sixties, for example, it became San Francisco's first all-talk station. And in 1968 KCBS broke new ground again when it adopted an all-news format, programming that would not only inform listeners but reflect the richness of the community and world they live in.

Much of the power behind KCBS' coverage, in fact, comes from the diversity and vividness of its news images, some of which the station repackaged in a series of taped anecdotes and observations produced for KCBS Newsradio's 20th Anniversary Celebration in 1988. Charles Kuralt led the series with

his recollections of the murders of Martin Luther King and Robert Kennedy in 1968. Walter Cronkite observed that history will likely show man's landing on the moon in 1969 to be the most important story of our lifetime. And Dan Rather remembered the Oval Office cover-up of 1972.

But the anniversary series also highlighted milestones in Bay Area history, as covered by KCBS: Willie Mays playing for the Giants, the assassinations in 1978 of Mayor George Moscone and Harvey Milk, the 49ers' 1982 Super Bowl victory, the happy exit from San Francisco Bay of Humphrey the Whale in 1985, and the 50th anniversary of the Golden Gate Bridge in 1987.

KCBS continues its mission of documenting the milestones and, equally important, keeping listeners in touch with the smaller everyday events, from traffic jams to rainstorms, that affect their lives. Twenty-four hours a day, KCBS is there, meeting listeners' expectations for clarity, consistency, and thoroughness.

KCBS Newsradio 74's newsroom covers all aspects of a breaking story.

PROFESSIONS

The business and professional community is an integral part of the city's infrastructure. By providing a wealth of service, expertise, and insight to the Bay Area, this sector enables continued growth and stability.

▲ Skadden, Arps, Slate, Meagher and Flom

▲ McCutchen, Doyle, Brown & Enersen

▲ Littler, Mendelson, Fastiff & Tichy

▲ Long & Levit ▲ Hallgrimson, McNichols, McCann & Inderbitzen

Photo by Barbara Filet/Tony Stone Worldwide

❏ ❏ ❏

SKADDEN, ARPS, SLATE, MEAGHER & FLOM

T he opening of Skadden, Arps, Slate, Meagher & Flom's San Francisco branch office in January 1987 linked the Bay Area to one of the world's premier full-service law firms.

Best known for its work in mergers and acquisitions, Skadden, Arps offers expertise in more than 25 other areas of law, including corporate finance, environmental law, commercial and securities litigation, antitrust law, tax law, and energy.

The firm was founded in 1948 in New York City, where it is still headquartered. The San Francisco office, which has grown from five to more than 40 lawyers, provides its clients access to the full range of Skadden, Arps' resources, which currently include more than 1,000 attorneys in seven U.S. and six foreign cities.

"Where expertise is required that we don't have here," says Ted Kozloff, partner at the San Francisco office, "our ability to access it is almost instantaneous." With Skadden, Arps offices in Los Angeles, Hong Kong, and Tokyo, Kozloff adds, the San Francisco branch is especially well-positioned to serve Bay Area clients with interests anywhere in California and throughout the Pacific Rim.

In addition to mergers and acquisitions, Skadden, Arps in San Francisco is very active in securities litigation and maintains a particularly strong environmental law practice, focusing on the environmental aspects of mergers and acquisitions as well as environmental-law compliance and litigation matters. Structured finance, a subspecialty of the firm's corporate-finance practice that handles securitization of financial assets, has emerged as another

of the San Francisco office's busiest practice areas.

Skadden, Arps' excellence in its wide range of specialties has attracted an impressive roster of clients, including more than one-third of the *Fortune* 500 industrial companies, all 10 of the world's largest banks, and almost every major U.S. investment bank.

Another component of the practice is pro bono work, to which the firm devotes substantial time and legal talent. In the Bay Area the firm's attorneys participate in pro bono matters such as emergency food programs, political asylum, and immigration proceedings. The result, of course, has been a strengthening of the link between the diverse Bay Area community and one of the world's premier full-service law firms.

LEFT: Skadden, Arps' San Francisco partners are (from left to right) Ted Kozloff (mergers and acquisitions), Phil Pollock (corporate and structured finance), Jim Lyons (securities litigation), and Jose Allen (environmental law).

McCutchen, Doyle, Brown & Enersen

McCutchen, Doyle, Brown & Enersen is one of the Bay Area's core institutions, a law firm that has consistently delivered high-quality legal services to business clients since its founding in San Francisco in 1883.

The McCutchen client of the late nineteenth century typically retained the firm for its expertise in admiralty law and municipal finance, or perhaps to defend a mining claim. Today the firm provides expertise in virtually all areas of business law, including commercial litigation, environmental, health care, intellectual property, international, real estate and land use, and corporate law. Just as significantly, McCutchen's growth and diversification have paralleled the Bay Area's expanding national and international interests and its increasingly important role in the global market.

Almost 300 McCutchen attorneys operate in San Francisco and in branch offices in San Jose, Walnut Creek, Los Angeles, Washington, D.C., and Taipei, as well as an affiliated office in Bangkok. All of these branch offices have been created since 1981, and during the same period the firm's staff more than doubled in size, facts that reflect McCutchen's commitment to serving the business community as it surges into global competition.

But going the extra distance in the name of service is not a recent innovation at McCutchen. It is a tradition. In 1899, when client Charles D. Lane purchased interests in mining claims in Nome, Alaska, McCutchen sent attorney

Samuel Knight to Nome to assist Lane as well as any others in the Yukon who might need legal services. In addition to establishing one of the very first law office branches in American history, Knight successfully defended Lane in a claims dispute.

And when the government of Taiwan lifted foreign exchange controls in 1987, McCutchen was there to help clients capitalize on new trade and investment opportunities. More recently, the firm's environmental practice group—one of the largest in the United States—has been serving as counsel to the Republic of China Environmental Protection Administration as it shapes environmental policy and legislation.

Founded by Charles Page and Charles Eells as Page & Eells, the firm has always embraced the inherent changeability of business, progressing through several partnership and name changes itself until 1967, when the current firm name was adopted. But even though partners have come and gone, the firm's devotion to service has not.

Throughout its history, McCutchen's willingness to accommodate clients' changing needs by increasing the range and depth of its services has kept it at the forefront of even the most highly technical aspects of business law. The firm's intellectual property group, for example, won the first case to hold that computer firmware may be copyrighted and assisted another client in successfully defending patents on recombinant DNA techniques. McCutchen also has added an in-house biophysicist and one of the nation's foremost copyright experts to augment its intellectual property practice.

As lead counsel to some of the world's largest financial institutions, McCutchen has assisted in dozens of multimillion-dollar loan transactions and helped both borrowers and lenders in designing creative financing instruments. To assist clients in Pacific Rim trade, McCutchen

The San Francsico head-
quarters of McCutchen,
Doyle, Brown & Enersen
in the Embarcadero
Center.
Inset: David R. Andrews,
McCutchen's managing
partner.

expanded to Taipei and affiliated with a
Bangkok firm. In Washington, D.C., the firm
focuses on legislative and administrative representation in environmental law, food and drug
law, and international trade. In California, the
firm built its land use practice into one of the
most versatile and efficient in the nation, representing developers in all aspects of land acquisition, entitlement, leasing, financing, and
construction.

Although its historical roots are in the Bay
Area, McCutchen's ties to the region and the
rest of California, in both professional and civic
capacities, are now stronger than ever. The San
Francisco headquarters is particularly well
known for its commercial transaction and
complex litigation practices. The firm's San Jose
office continues to grow with the high-tech
environment of Silicon Valley and also
represents many clients in San Jose's expanded
federal court system. And while the Walnut
Creek office continues to develop its highly regarded land use practice, the Los Angeles office
focuses on commercial litigation and
environmental and health care law.

Like all community-minded Bay Area

businesses, McCutchen combines pragmatic dis-
cipline, creative energy, and diversity in nurtur-
ing community relationships. More than one-
third of the firm's attorneys are women, and
many have held executive positions in
professions other than law before joining
McCutchen. Many of the attorneys express
enthusiasm for their communities through
civic involvement.

One partner in the Walnut Creek office was
instrumental in the fund-raising and planning
for that city's recently completed Regional Center for the Arts. Other McCutchen attorneys
have served as mayors, city council members,
and presidents of state and local bar associations.

McCutchen's lawyers also assist AIDS
patients, people who are homeless, battered
women, and political refugees, among others,
with more than 10,000 hours of pro bono work
each year. The firm was recently honored for
this work by the California Rural Assistance
Foundation and the State Bar of California,
which awarded McCutchen's San Jose office the
"President's Public Service Award" for "extraordinary provision of pro bono legal services to
the poor."

Littler, Mendelson, Fastiff & Tichy

Many law firms grow by adding practice specialties. Littler, Mendelson, Fastiff & Tichy has grown by focusing exclusively on one specialty—employment law.

Littler, Mendelson has been providing high-quality and timely legal services to employers since its founding in 1942. But demand for these services has increased dramatically in recent years as the array of employment regulations has become wider and more complex.

The field of employment law has, in fact, grown into one of the legal profession's broadest and most diverse specialties. Partner Arthur Mendelson notes that while the firm consisted of six attorneys when he joined it in 1944, today the practice has more than 175 lawyers among 420 employees overall, making it the largest single-specialty law firm in the United States.

The focus of Littler, Mendelson's employment law practice has also shifted significantly since its founding. Although employer-union problems continue, because the percentage of unionized employees nationwide is significantly less than it was in 1960, employer-union problems have been overtaken by issues generated by employers' legal relationships with individual employees. And while Littler, Mendelson does extensive work before administrative agencies such as the National Labor Relations Board, in-creasing attention is now paid to issues such as wrongful discharge litigation, employee benefits, employee privacy rights, drug abuse in the workplace, and equal employment opportunity litigation.

Although Littler, Mendelson represents employers in virtually every industry, including many *Fortune* 500 corporations, a large percentage of the firm's clients are small and mid-size companies. Some of these clients have no more than five employees, while some have 500. No single client accounts for more than 3 percent of the firm's billings.

The pool of clients has also become more diverse. Since the mid-1980s the firm's client base has increasingly reflected the Bay Area's links to businesses throughout the Pacific Rim. "As [international] companies learn more about how law works in the United States," says partner Garry Mathiason, "they learn it's to their advantage to have a specialist in the field of employment law."

Mathiason recalls a recent case in which Littler, Mendelson led a Japanese client, who had no previous experience as an employer in the United States, through the legal steps needed to hire its first 100 employees in this country. Virtually every aspect of the legal relationship between employer and employee was covered, from the basics of designing an employee payroll

(Left to right) George Tichy, Arthur Mendelson, and Wesley Fastiff in the firm's headquarters office.

to writing an employee handbook, from determining appropriate interview questions to deciding whether or not to do drug testing.

Another emerging area of the practice is its preventive education program, which is aimed at assisting client companies in developing sound employment practices that will enhance employer-employee relations and help avoid litigation.

A popular feature of this preventive-education program is the "breakfast briefing," a two-hour morning meeting during which Littler, Mendelson attorneys review and explain the practical ramifications of new employment legislation. Participants also receive a manual on the new legislation to supplement the lecture.

The popularity of these breakfast briefings (one series on the Americans With Disabilities Act was attended by more than 1,000 people) is due in part to the fact that that they are concise, cost-efficient alternatives to the two-day legal review seminars commonly used by many corporations. Also, Littler, Mendelson's seminars—along with the rest of its

preventive-education programs—resonate with the larger economic concerns of many businesses.

"One of the things this education component has responded to," says Littler, Mendelson partner Barbara de Oddone, "is the concern to keep legal costs down. That fits very well with our effort to give people practical advice about how to avoid litigation."

To facilitate delivery of these programs, as well as the full range of Littler, Mendelson services, the firm has expanded beyond its San Francisco headquarters into four additional Bay Area offices (Menlo Park, San Jose, Santa Rosa, and Walnut Creek), eight offices in other parts of California, and branches in New Orleans, Baltimore, Portland, and Washington, D.C.

This nationwide expansion, Mathiason adds, is also a response to the increasing number of corporations seeking the best specialized outside resources. "We fit perfectly with the needs of a corporation that doesn't necessarily go to one law firm for all purposes," he says, "but looks for the best advice available."

Long & Levit

Long & Levit is the largest litigation law firm in the San Francisco Bay Area. Founded in 1927 by former San Francisco city attorney Percy Long and Bert Levit, the firm's practice initially and for many years focused on the representation and counseling of insurance-industry executives and their companies in insurance matters.

A dramatic shift in the firm's work occurred in 1975 when partner Ronald Mallen published his book *Legal Malpractice*. In the context of the mid-1970s, the timing of that publication was auspicious. Sentiments against lawyers had been aroused by the Watergate scandal. The rise of consumerism and decline in the mystique of the legal professional

real estate and insurance agents and brokers.

Currently, the fastest growing segment of the practice is environmental coverage litigation, a subspecialty of the insurance-coverage litigation services that Long & Levit has been providing to insurance companies for more than 60 years. The main issue: Will comprehensive general-liability insurance policies cover policyholders' participation in pollution cleanups mandated by state and federal agencies? Relatively few court opinions have been delivered on the subject so far. But because of their leading roles in several major environmental cases, the firm's growing team of environmental coverage attorneys are at the forefront in clarifying policy applications and resolving environmental coverage disputes.

Long & Levit's expansive lobby on the 23rd floor of 101 California Street doubles as the firm's library, a well-attended centerpiece that sets the tone for the rest of the office.

produced an explosion of litigation against attorneys.

Recognized as the definitive work on legal malpractice, Mallen's treatise prompted the development of the firm's present concentration on litigation in general and the defense of legal professionals sued for malpractice in particular. This transformation was far-reaching enough to earn Long & Levit preeminence in dozens of other civil litigation specialties.

The firm's national prominence in legal malpractice, for example, has been bolstered by its malpractice defense work for a broad range of other professionals, including accountants, physicians, dentists, corporate directors and officers, commodities and securities brokers, and

The firm's resume also includes specialties such as corporate directors and officers insurance, product liability, and banking litigation. General commercial litigation, which includes construction litigation and white-collar criminal work, is another growing area. There is even a small maritime law group that includes among its clients the San Francisco Bar Pilots.

Even though many of its clients are headquartered elsewhere, most of Long & Levit's attorneys are located in the firm's main office, on two floors at 101 California Street in downtown San Francisco. The more than 80 lawyers serving the practice today are operating on a scale far different from that of the practice founded 65 years ago.

The expansive lobby on the 23rd floor of 101 California Street doubles as Long & Levit's library, a well-attended centerpiece that sets the tone for the rest of the office. Immediately upon entering, clients and visitors know that they are in the midst of an active law firm. State-of-the-art computer technology provides up-to-date litigation support for the firm's attorneys and staff. The firm's quarterly publication, "Legal Malpractice Report," links subscribers to the latest in malpractice-prevention strategies, legal ethics, and related litigation and insurance developments. A fully equipped courtroom used by the firm for training and trial preparation is the focal point of the firm's conference center.

Until the mid-1970s the staple of the founding partners' practice—representation of people who formed and owned insurance companies and agencies—sustained the careers of about eight attorneys in San Francisco, plus a small group of lawyers in a Los Angeles branch office that the firm opened in 1947. From 1976 to 1979, as the impact of Ronald Mallen's book changed the direction of the firm, Long & Levit grew to 42 lawyers. In 1983 the practice was fully reorganized, with all non-litigating partners and the Los Angeles office departing the firm. In 1992 the firm again opened a Los Angeles office to meet the increasing demand by its clients for a Long & Levit presence in Southern California.

A tour of Long & Levit today shows a still-growing practice that takes pride in its identity.

The firm's connection to the Bay Area is strengthened by its lawyers' history of civic, as well as professional, commitments. Before cofounding the firm, Percy Long had been city attorney of San Francisco for 12 years. Bert Levit served as state finance director under Governor Edmund G. Brown and as a prominent member of the San Francisco Board of Education.

Long & Levit lawyers, legal assistants, and staff carry on this tradition of civic involvement— in government, politics, and the arts. They also provide pro bono assistance for immigrants, the homeless, and other underserved groups. The result is a blend of professional diversity and community support that fits Long & Levit's identity perfectly.

State-of-the-art computer technology provides up-to-date litigation support for the firm's attorneys and staff.

A fully equipped courtroom used by Long & Levit for training and trial preparation is the focal point of the firm's conference center.

HALLGRIMSON, MCNICHOLS, MCCANN & INDERBITZEN

In January 1991 two well-established law practices merged to form one of the most highly respected Bay Area firms specializing in real estate law and business litigation. That firm—Hallgrimson, McNichols, McCann & Inderbitzen—carries on a tradition of legal service begun in the Amador Valley before the turn of the century and in the Santa Clara Valley in the 1960s.

There are few firms in the southern part of the Bay Area with Hallgrimson, McNichols' history of success and depth of experience. Providing cost-effective service tailored to each client's needs, Hallgrimson, McNichols offers expertise in all aspects of real estate transactions, including joint ventures, financing, development, government approval, land use, acquisitions, construction, leasing, dispositions, and exchanges. The practice also includes business and tax planning, general business and commercial matters, and business and real estate litigation.

By way of developing one of the best reputations in real estate law in Northern California, the firm has served some of the Bay Area's most successful real estate developers, nonprofit housing developers, domestic and foreign lenders, investors, commercial tenants, real estate brokers, contractors, electronics and technology

Steve McNichols and Steve Hallgrimson, two partners in the firm, on the steps of the courthouse in San Jose.

Howard S. Miller, partner; Steven Fleisher, partner; Nickolas Tooliatos, partner; and Celine Duke, associate, in the office library.

companies, and various government entities.

The firm's litigation group, headed by Steve McNichols, has been a leader in complex business litigation in the East Bay since the early 1970s. Known for its creative and efficient service to the business community, the litigation group provides sophisticated advice for decision-making, the legal documentation and strategy to implement those decisions, and effective litigation support to resolve legal disputes.

The founding partners of the firm envisioned a dynamic firm that would keep pace with the needs and growth of their clients in the South Bay and East Bay. Their goal has been to establish a full-service law firm that provides superior, individualized service. The goal has largely been realized: Hallgrimson, McNichols is one of the

fastest growing legal practices in the region, serving clients from its offices at 5000 Hopyard Road, Suite 400, Pleasanton, and 40 South Market Street, Suite 700, San Jose.

This growth has been fostered by the firm's experience in real estate transactions, including joint ventures, financing, development, governmental approvals, land use, acquisitions, construction, leasing, dispositions, and exchanges.

Although it continues to expand its client base, Hallgrimson, McNichols' is committed to a core philosophy of looking beyond standard solutions to build one-on-one relationships that inspire trust and confidence, and of identifying the most efficient and cost-effective way to resolve an issue.

FROM THE GROUND UP

 s a metropolitan leader, the Bay Area is constantly redefining its horizons with a look to the future. With this vision in mind, architects, developers, and realtors work together to enrich the city's skyline and preserve its integrity.

▲ DES Architects + Engineers
▲ Rubicon Property Services ▲ Reynolds
& Brown ▲ Embarcadero Center
▲ The Doric Group

Photo by Mark E. Gibson

❏ ❏ ❏

DES Architects + Engineers

LEFT TOP: Plaza Ramona, Palo Alto. Photo by Steve Whittaker

LEFT BOTTOM: First Deposit National Corporation, Pleasanton. Photo by Jane Lidz

MIDDLE TOP: Chips and Technologies Campus, San Jose. Photo by Vittoria

RIGHT TOP AND BOTTOM: Claris, Ireland. Photo by Blake-Hastings

Buildings designed by DES Architects + Engineers are products of a collaborative effort between client and architect, thoughtful combinations of aesthetic tone and engineering logic, and models of function and visual energy.

The First Nationwide Bank Campus in Sacramento, The Pacific Athletic Club at Redwood Shores, Chips & Technologies in San Jose, Plaza Ramona in Palo Alto, HMT in Fremont, First Deposit National Corporation in Pleasanton, and Cooper House in Santa Cruz—each of these DES-designed buildings uniquely integrates creative expression with practical need.

Based in Redwood City, with a branch office in Fremont, DES has applied its expertise throughout the western United States and internationally. The Bay Area, however, is home to DES's broadest range of work, from low- and mid-rise office buildings to R&D, manufacturing, health care, educational, and retail projects.

Whatever the project, DES has unfailingly balanced its standards of quality service and cost effectiveness with creativity.

When Apple Computer sought DES's services in designing its Logistics Campus in Northern California, DES worked with its usual commitment to client-architect collaboration and problem solving. The result: Apple's requirements and vision for the campus were transformed into reality through DES's client sensitivity and professional expertise.

DES also provides unsurpassed project management services, from programming to schematic design to construction administration, and maintains positive and productive relationships with the builders of its designs.

The best recommendations for these services, of course, come from satisfied clients, of which DES has no shortage. Claris vice president Randy Komisar praised DES's "understanding of our company and its needs" in redesigning Claris' Santa Clara headquarters. Apple Computer Inc.'s development, design, and construction director, Robert McIntire, expressed deep satisfaction with DES Architects + Engineers' "thoughtful, economical, and creative" approach in designing Apple facilities in Sacramento and in Cork, Ireland. Larry D. McReynolds, facilities manager at Triad Systems Corporation, called the DES-designed Triad campus facility in Livermore "the pride of Livermore and ... the standard by which all projects are judged."

RUBICON PROPERTY SERVICES

Comprehensive property management is Rubicon Property Services' principal product. Client confidence is its principal byproduct.

Based in San Francisco, Rubicon provides a broad range of real estate services for commercial, retail, and industrial properties. And because it focuses exclusively on Bay Area properties, Rubicon's performance-oriented program of management services is optimally tailored to the regional market.

The firm, founded in 1987, touts its narrow geographic focus and relatively small size as advantages over large, national companies with huge staffs. Rubicon thrives on teamwork. Its exceptionally well-trained professionals take pride in their ability to efficiently formulate and coordinate a marketing strategy and multidisciplinary management program for each property they handle.

The key is the diversity of Rubicon's expertise. Property management, notes Rubicon president Robert A. Bagguley, has long since expanded beyond the realm of mere rent collecting and building maintenance. Rubicon's menu of services, for example, includes project marketing and consulting services, property managment, due diligence research for clients on prospective real estate purchases, and strategic repositioning of foreclosed properties.

In addition, Rubicon has established a subsidiary, Trafalgar Construction, which offers a full range of construction services, from consulting to general contracting. Although Trafalgar provides services to many customers not on Rubicon's client list, Bagguley sees it as a perfect—often essential—complement to sufficient property management.

"Being a property manager," observes Bagguley, "we look at doing our general contracting a little bit differently than most general contractors. In other words, we like to come in at the very beginning and pre-program a tenant's needs, represent the tenant directly in coordinating all the subcontractors."

This marriage of general contracting and property management also facilitates such things as selection of an architect (some specialize in law offices, some in banks, some in high-tech design, and so on); supervision of improvements so that they comply with regulatory and safety requirements; and formulation and supervision of preventive-maintenance programs.

In recognition of the fact that many of the firm's clients—which include major insurance companies, financial institutions, and off-shore clients throughout the Pacific Rim—prefer more than standard monthly financial reports, Rubicon provides worldwide access, via computer modem, to its financial data bank, updated meticulously each day.

To date, Rubicon has focused heavily on turning around and managing distressed properties acquired by institutional clients. As he looks ahead, Bagguley believes Rubicon will continue to attract institutional clients aware of the firm's comprehensive approach to managing and marketing these properties.

"I feel that this is part of our forte," says Bagguley. "We are very good at seeing what needs to be done at a property and repositioning it to where a client can sell it and then focus on another."

Rubicon Property Services' computer-reporting system instantly provides clients with up-to-date financial information, accessible from anywhere in the world.

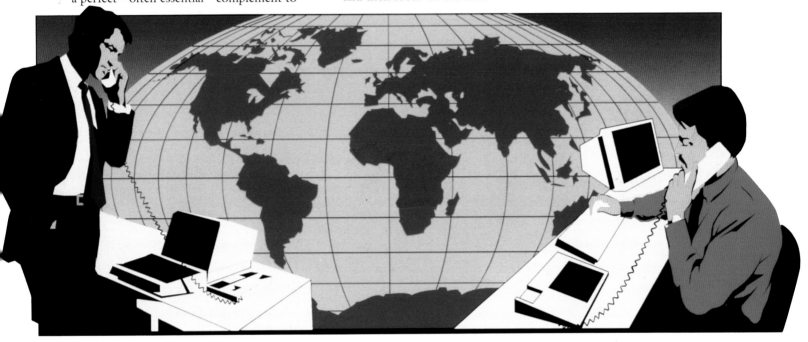

REYNOLDS & BROWN

Reynolds & Brown is improving the Bay Area landscape one commercial development project at a time.

A deteriorating school district property in the East Bay is transformed into a thriving promotional retail center. A 155,000-square-foot home furnishing and improvement center, anchored by The Home Depot, attracts shoppers to Pleasanton. Space in a 43,000-square-foot office/industrial park in San Leandro is virtually sold out before the park's completion.

Each of these Reynolds & Brown projects is a financial success. Each is a high-quality, well-designed facility. Each also is a showcase for Reynolds & Brown's ability to work with local communities in shaping projects that meet regional needs.

Reynolds & Brown is, by definition, a local company. Based in Concord, the firm operates exclusively in the East Bay, which also is home to all of its employees. The company's diverse range of mid-size commercial projects are sprinkled throughout Alameda, Contra Costa, and Solano counties. Yet, the projects all fall within easy distance to manage and supervise with local employees, a unique factor of the company.

The company's commitment to maintaining its local identity dovetails with its conscientious approach to development. Reynolds & Brown employees are civically active. Some do volunteer work; some, such as the company cofounder Jon Reynolds, serve on regional boards and commissions. Reynolds's civic resume is particularly impressive: he has served as a trustee of the Urban Land Institute, a commissioner on the Oakland/Alameda County Coliseum Board, chairman of the Oakland Housing Foundation, and chairman of the board of directors of the East Bay Municipal Utility District.

Community involvement is one of the firm's main organizational values, the backbone of the commitment to planning, developing, and maintaining projects that will create long-term community benefit as well as good real estate value.

"We have always focused on projects where there is a reason to build a building," says Reynolds & Brown president Thomas Terrill. "So we tend to do projects that we think will stand the test of time in terms of

functional design and application."

Although Reynolds & Brown officially was established as a corporation in 1967, Jon Reynolds and David Brown actually began co-developing Bay Area real estate in 1963. Their early projects, built in the 1960s and 1970s, were industrial, distribution, and sales and service facilities. In the 1980s they added research and development projects and office buildings to their portfolio. More recently, the firm has produced off-price retail projects, such as Marina Square Promotional Center, a 155,000-square-foot San Leandro shopping center anchored by Nordstrom Rack, Marshalls, BizMart, Gap Outlet, and Eddie Bauer Outlet.

The diversity of these developments has enhanced the firm's proficiency in resolving com-

plex entitlement and land use issues. The Marina Square project, for example, is on the former site of Pacific High School, closed in the mid-1980s by the school district because of declining enrollment. Working in partnership with civic entities, Reynolds & Brown helped develop an infrastructure improvement plan for redevelopment of the site. Merging private financing with funds from a county-approved sales tax, road improvements were made and the $25-million retail center was built.

"The project generates more than $500,000 annually in sales tax for the city, a great deal of money for the school district from the sales, and has provided an environment for our tenants to succeed," observes Terrill. "Our job was to take a myriad of problems, pose solutions, and focus the energy to make it happen." The company also

recognizes that its ability to solve complicated entitlement issues is useful only if its projects are both attractive to tenants and profitable for Reynolds & Brown. So far, the firm's projects have consistently met both requirements. Reynolds & Brown is strongly market driven, explains Terrill, noting that in 30 years the company shifted from industrial to office to retail development in direct response to market change. Its focus continues to be on well-located parcels of land, shaping the ultimate buildings to the market.

Because of the firm's broad, multidisciplinary experience in the East Bay, Terrill sees Reynolds & Brown doing more property and asset management, particularly for clients unfamiliar with the East Bay market. As always, there will also be new projects—well placed, well designed, successful, and enhancements to their communities.

ABOVE: Marina Square, a value-oriented shopping center developed by Reynolds & Brown in San Leandro.

TOP: Pleasanton Square, a retail center developed by Reynolds & Brown in Pleasanton, focuses on home improvement-related tenants such as Home Depot.

EMBARCADERO CENTER

RIGHT: Embarcadero Center's building lighting has become a San Francisco tradition welcoming the holiday season.

E mbarcadero Center is one of the biggest real estate success stories in the Bay Area.

What was known as the Barbary Coast during the mid-1800s is now San Francisco's most impressive mixed-use commercial development. Begun in 1968, the project now includes five high-rise office towers, more than 140 restaurants and retail shops, the historic Federal Reserve Bank Building, and two high-rise hotels with a combined capacity of approximately 1,200 guest rooms. The entire complex is accessed by tree-lined pedestrian walkways, artistically landscaped public areas, and parking facilities for 2,400 vehicles.

The combination of practical convenience, meticulously maintained facilities, aesthetics, and prestige (the towers offer some of the region's most spectacular views) has made an Embarcadero Center lease among the financial district's most sought-after. The entire complex houses approximately 12,000 workers and approximately 300 tenants in more than 3.4 million square feet of office space, all of it expertly managed by Pacific Property Services.

Tenant spaces range in size from 1,000 square feet to more than an entire floor. Law firms such as McCutchen, Doyle, Brown & Enersen and Orrick, Herrington & Sutcliffe have Embarcadero Center addresses. The advertising firm J. Walter Thompson is a tenant, as are Peat Marwick Main & Co., National Union Fire Insurance Co., Industrial Indemnity Co., and Marsh & McClennan Inc.

Shops such as The Gap, Ann Taylor, Williams-Sonoma, Pottery Barn, Victoria's Secret, The Nature Company, The Limited, and Limited Express fill the three retail levels. The retail mix is completed by top-line restaurants, including Splendido, Harbor Village Restaurant, Chevys Mexican Restaurant, Pizzeria Uno, and Scott's Seafood Grill & Bar.

As THE major landlord of office space in downtown San Francisco, Embarcadero Center is in a position to offer tenants an unusually high degree of flexibility in meeting expansion needs. When space is not available all in one building, it is found elsewhere in the complex. Embarcadero Center is also equipped to handle build-out needs for both office and retail tenants.

Because of its abundance of high-quality retail amenities and prime hotel accommodations, Embarcadero Center is one of the few locations in San Francisco's financial district that also has become a destination for tourists. The series of five office towers along Sacramento Street is anchored by a hotel at each end, the 360-room Park Hyatt at Battery Street and the 804-room Hyatt Regency at California Street. The hotels are also at the hub of public-transporation services (including MUNI and BART rail lines) and within minutes of the Moscone Convention Center and tourist destinations such as Fisherman's Wharf.

Three levels of open-air, tree-lined plazas are interconnected by pedestrian walkways spanning city streets.

Well known as San Francisco's most prestigious office address, Embarcadero Center is also known for its award-winning landscaping and public art collection.

The financial district's metamorphosis from a waterfront full of saloons, gold-seekers, and shipping companies to landfill hosting most stunning multi-use commercial developments has included a few transformations in between. Prior to the population explosion sparked by the gold rush, which began in 1849, San Francisco's northeastern waterfront began where Montgomery Street is today—several blocks west of Embarcadero Center. By May 1959, when city supervisors adopted the Golden Gateway Redevelopment Plan for the eight-block area, landfill projects had pushed the shoreline into its current profile. The reason for the redevelopment plan: the area had become a rundown produce and warehouse district.

In their bid to the redevelopment agency, John Portman and Associates, David Rockefeller and Associates, and Trammel Crow Development proposed a master-planned commercial project designed to revive the area with an innovative mix of office, retail, and hotel uses. Before the project got underway in 1968, Prudential Property Co. had replaced Trammel Crow in the owner-developer trio, which proceeded to develop Embarcadero Center in three phases.

Phase I—opened for operation in 1971—consists of One Embarcadero Center and the Hyatt Regency Hotel. Phase II—completed by 1981—put Embarcadero Center Towers Two, Three, and Four on the downtown skyline. The third phase, called Embarcadero Center West, combined construction of the Park Hyatt Hotel, renovation of the Federal Reserve Bank Building into office space (the building retains its historic-landmark status), and completion of the Embarcadero Center West Tower. This

final phase was completed in 1989.

But Embarcadero Center's owner representatives have set a precedent for mixed-used innovation and have a knack for keeping the project current. The Embarcadero Center's public-area renovation project launched in April 1991, for example, features office-tower lobbies redesigned to include two-story vaulted ceilings, a dramatic increase in natural and artificial lighting, a comprehensive signage and graphics program, enhanced landscaping, and individually designed storefronts.

The four-year improvement program, says Pacific Property Services senior vice president Herb Lembcke, "will help maintain an innovative and fresh environment that will better serve the people who work, shop, and seek entertainment at the center."

A popular destination for tourists and residents alike, Embarcadero Center features more than 140 fashionable shops and restaurants.

THE DORIC GROUP

ABOVE: Ronald H. Cowan, chairman of The Doric Group.

RIGHT: Harbor Bay's ideal climate and campus-like setting combine to create a comfortable work environment.

BELOW: Harbor Bay's setting, on the eastern shore of San Francisco Bay, includes this spectacular view of San Francisco.

Dynamic collaboration between industry and academic research is paving the way for an array of new biotechnology products. Observers cite the Doric Group's Harbor Bay Business and Research Park in Alameda, as a potential "biomedical Silicon Valley," a place where scientific discovery can quickly find practical application. Harbor Bay's ample developable land can immediately accommodate facilities for new ventures between businesses and some of the world's most highly-respected research institutions.

Harbor Bay Business and Research Park is part of Harbor Bay Isle, an award-winning, 1,000-acre planned community. In 1992 more than 70 research, office, and commercial enterprises were housed in the park. Several were sole tenants of handsome custom-designed buildings and others occupied the park's five tastefully-landscaped multitenant building clusters.

All development entitlements are in place for the Park's remaining 200 acres of improved, virgin, toxic-free-land—the rarest of Metropolitan Bay Area real estate commodities. This means that new research and development ventures can occupy custom-constructed buildings in under 18 months.

Harbor Bay Village's 3,000-plus homes are clustered in small, highly livable neighborhoods. There are bike and jogging paths, neighborhood parks and swimming pools, lagoons, trees, and flowers. Three daycare centers serve Business and Research Park

tenants as well as residents.

The Harbor Bay Business and Research Park lies dead center between University of California/Davis, Stanford University, University of California/San Francisco, University of California/Berkeley, and Lawrence Berkeley and Lawrence Livermore. These institutions together comprise the largest critical mass of research

activities of any region in the world. Harbor Bay Isle's central location is ideally suited for the collaborative research activities being initiated by these major research institutions.

In short, Harbor Bay Isle is poised to play a major role in the evolution of the Bay Area and, ultimately, in the global economics of biomedical research and development.

Geographically, Harbor Bay isle is at the center of the nine-county Bay Area. Harbor Bay is served by the Interstate 80/880 corridor and is linked by shuttle service to the Bay Area Rapid Transit

(BART) light-rail system. The park is five minutes from the Oakland International Airport and just south of the Port of Oakland, one of the West Coast's busiest and best-equipped container ports.

Since Harbor Bay lies directly on San Francisco Bay, it operates its own high-speed ferry service to and from downtown San Francisco. As highways become ever more conjested, the Bay will serve as an increasingly important transportation spine. Harbor Bay is poised to link itself to all parts of the Bay via high-speed ferry service.

Augmenting this efficient infrastructure is

Superior architecture and landscaping are hallmarks of Harbor Bay.

BELOW: The Harbor Bay teleport's microwave tower has become a symbol of Harbor Bay's commitment to technological innovation.

Harbor Bay Telecommunications. Harbor Bay Telecommunications is the Doric Group's provider of fully-integrated communications products and services to Business and Research Park tenants.

Harbor Bay Isle is home to the control center of the Bay Area Teleport. The Teleport is a regional microwave and fiber-optic distribution network, and proprietary earth-station satellite service. The Teleport provides a package of communications services with vast voice and data transmission capabilities.

One of Harbor Isle's most attractive features is space to grow. In 1992 the Doric Group held entitlements for 4.3 million square feet of new research and development space. Under Doric's flexible development strategy, corporations and institutions may purchase, lease, or build-to-suit. Parcels range from 10,000 square feet to 20 or more acres.

Environmental and recreational opportunities abound in the Harbor Bay Isle community. There are 45 holes of golf, and 17 miles of walking, jogging, and cycling trails winding through greenbelts and along shoreline parks and lagoons. The Harbor Bay Club features tennis, swimming, a fitness center, and restaurants. At every turn are the spectacular vistas of the Bay and the San Francisco skyline.

Harbor Bay Isle is a rare treasure. A master-planned community of such magnitude and beauty, offering such superb quality of life, located directly on San Francisco Bay in the exact center of the Metropolitan Bay Area, could never again be recreated and permitted in today's complex society.

ABOVE: The Harbor Bay Club is a 10-acre facility that includes a wide range of recreational amenities.

LEFT: Harbor Bay's residential development includes some of the Bay Area's finest housing stock.

Harbor Bay's recreational amenities include numerous waterways.

MARKETPLACE

ay Area residents and visitors alike can partake of a variety of services within this cultural mecca. Retail establishments and hotels offer unique and quality experiences.

▲ Parc Fifty Five ▲ Hotel DeAnza

▲ San Mateo County Expo Center

▲ Casa Madrona Hotel and Restaurant

▲ California Parlor Car Tours

▲ Nob Hill Lambourne ▲ The Showplace

Square Group ▲ Nestlé Beverage Company

▲ Consolidated Freightways, Inc.

Photo by Roger Allyn Lee/The Photo File

❏ ❏ ❏

Parc Fifty Five

Just three blocks from Moscone Convention Center, two blocks from Union Square shopping, and one block from the theater district, Parc Fifty Five occupies one of the choicest locations in downtown San Francisco.

But its location is only the foundation for Parc Fifty Five's success. Its guests are not only in the middle of the action, they are among the best-attended guests in town, thanks to a commitment to service by Parc Fifty Five's owners, Hong Kong's Chan family, who owns and manages a growing international chain of hotels and real estate holdings.

After more than 20 years of successful hotel and real estate ventures in the crown colony, the Chan family opened Parc Fifty Five—Park Lane's first hotel in the United States—on October 1, 1984. The hotel has emerged as one of the most impressive links in the Park Lane

ABOVE: Parc Fifty Five combines Asian hospitality, European tradition, and American technology in catering to an international clientele.

chain, capitalizing on San Francisco's stature as a West Coast financial center and capturing some of the highest occupancy rates in the city since 1987.

Initially operating under the name and management of Ramada Renaissance, the hotel was brought under Park Lane management and renamed Parc Fifty Five in May 1989. The hotel has targeted the corporate traveler and upscale-tourist markets, estimating that about 70 percent of Parc Fifty Five's business comes from business travelers, and the balance from vacationers.

A compact-looking stepped exterior disguises the fact that the 32-story hotel contains 1,006 guest rooms, two restaurants, two cocktail lounges, a health club, and almost 20,000 square feet of meeting facilities. Staffed by about 650 people, Parc Fifty Five offers all bay-window views from each room.

"The ultimate pampering," is offered in the Concierge Club, the 50 guest rooms and 15 suites on the top four floors of the hotel. Concierge Club amenities include private-elevator access, private check-in, panoramic views, breakfast brought to the room, and a special staff to assist with such things as dinner reservations and theater tickets.

This wide range of amenities and devotion to good service are at the heart of the identity that Park Lane is creating for all its hotels, including the 390-room Coco Palms Resort on Kauai, Hawaii; the 452-room Churchill in London; the 314-room Fountain Suites in Phoenix; the 488-room Oakland in California; the 580-room ParkLane in Sydney, Australia; the 350-room St. Anthony in San Antonio, Texas; and the 850-room Park Lane, the company's flagship hotel in Hong Kong.

The diversity of these properties in both size and appearance is no accident—the Chan family has taken special care with its hotels to avoid the cookie-cutter sameness common to many chains. And yet each hotel maintains a distinctive continuity of service and ambience: Park Lane markets a unique, multicultural style of service that emphasizes the best elements of Asian hospitality, European tradition, and American technology.

At the helm of the family's San Francisco-based international operations is Lawrence Chan, trained by his father in the hotel and real estate businesses from childhood. Although

Lawrence Chan was only 31 when he presided over the 1984 opening of Parc Fifty Five, he had long since assimilated the Chan family business acumen and its vision for international expansion.

One key to Lawrence Chan's business philosophy is his long-term commitment to his hotel and other real estate holdings. These properties, Chan has said, were not purchased for quick profits.

Not surprisingly, many of these enterprises carry the burden of intense community involvement. The $120-million Oakland Chinatown redevelopment project, for example, was award-

ed to Chan's development company, C&L Financial Inc., in spite of competition from several local developers. The project has in fact brought Chan into the ranks of civic and business leaders committed to making Oakland a culturally and commercjally thriving, world-class city.

Meanwhile, Chan must maintain a global perspective toward sustaining Park Lane's growth. With the backing of about 200 investors, including Japan Airlines, Standard Charter Bank of London, and Maru Beni Trading Co. of Japan, Chan has his company comfortably on course in establishing hotels in the major financial centers of the world.

The roster of Park Lane hotels includes locations in cities such as Hong Kong, London, and San Francisco and the Park Lane Sydney in Australia.Further acquisitions are being considered in cities such as Bangkok, Singapore, and Taipei. And with each new property will come growing appreciation of the Asian hospitality, European tradition, and American technology with which Park Lane cares for its guests.

HOTEL DEANZA

RIGHT: From the original Jazz Age neon sign on the roof to its figured friezes, Hotel DeAnza's renovated exterior looks virtually identical to the 1930s DeAnza original.

The 1990 grand reopening of the restored Hotel DeAnza, built in downtown San Jose in 1931, reintroduced the public to an architectural treasure and one of the Bay Area's finest hotels.

Hotel DeAnza's renovated exterior looks virtually identical to the 1930s DeAnza original, from its figured friezes to the original Jazz Age neon sign on the roof. Owner-developer Saratoga Capital Inc., of San Jose, hired local architecture firm Kenneth Rodriguez & Assoc. and contractor Barry Swenson, grandson of the hotel's original builder, to round out a development team that began work on the property in early 1989.

The inside of the 100-room Hotel DeAnza, affectionately known as the "Grand Lady of San Jose," is completely new. San Francisco-based interior designer, Joszi Meskan Associates, has created an atmosphere that is at once sensual and homelike, a combination of art deco geometric simplicity, rich natural colors, and modern convenience.

Originally designed by architect William Weeks, the DeAnza retains plenty of its original romantic charm as well as its top-floor view of the Mt. Diablo range. The improvements skillfully capitalize on the hotel's Spanish Renaissance and modern themes without a hint of pretentiousness. Custom fixtures such as etched-glass chandeliers, figured doors, and floral carpets carry the art deco mood throughout the building. It is luxurious without ever seeming overwhelming, a showcase of comfort and good taste.

"We tried to blend as much of the historical, Old World kind of feeling as we could with all of the modern conveniences," says DeAnza general manager David Lautensack. "We tried to blend it in such a way so that it has a very comfortable, residential feel, so that it's not ostentatious."

Listed on the National Registry of Historical Places, the DeAnza is located at Santa Clara Street and Almaden Boulevard, gateway to downtown San Jose's recently refurbished business district. The 10-story building,

The cornerstone of Hotel DeAnza's appeal to business patrons is a special, informal food service that makes busy guests feel at home.

renovated at a cost of $12 million, is within three blocks of the new San Jose Convention Center and is two blocks from the Center of the Performing Arts and the San Jose Arena, now under construction. The hotel is also within 10 minutes of the San Jose International Airport.

The DeAnza is marketed primarily to business travelers, although it also attracts a substantial number of vacationers, local organizations, and special events. The DeAnza's facilities and approach to service, in fact, cater to a wide range of clientele.

For the business traveler, the hotel provides a working desk, multiple-line phone with voice mail message service, dedicated data line and FAX port, armoire honor bar, two televisions (one in the bathroom), and a VCR in each of its rooms. Upon request, the hotel also will provide computers and FAX machines in guest rooms. The DeAnza's meeting facilities can accommodate everything from corporate board meetings to gatherings of 100 people. To supplement those meetings, the hotel has full audiovisual and teleconferencing capabilities.

The cornerstone of Hotel DeAnza's appeal to business patrons is a special, informal food service that makes busy guests feel at home. Breakfast, lunch, and dinner are served in a contemporary Italian restaurant, La Pastaia. The Hedley Club Room provides cocktails and live entertainment, while the Palm Court is the perfect setting for outdoor gatherings. And to assuage their late-night hunger, guests are invited to "Raid the Pantry" in the hotel dining room and help themselves to a selection of complimentary sandwiches and snacks.

The Raid the Pantry concept, adds Lautensack, is among the hotel's most unusual and popular amenities. "It's one of the most important things we offer as far as making guests feel at home," he says, "one of the things that sets us apart from other hotels."

Painstaking care is taken to provide guests with a level of service that is truly unique. The hotel's *Exclusively Yours*^{sm} program offers special amenities and services too numerous to mention. The De Anza's *Guest of Honor*^{sm} program rewards frequent guests with even greater personalized service. The hotel's International Guest Assistance Program caters to the special needs of its international travelers.

The resurrection of the property is all the more impressive considering its recent history: Like downtown San Jose itself, the hotel had spent the past few decades in decline. Business dropped off in the 1960s and 1970s in the downtown area as merchants left for the suburbs, and the DeAnza's condition was symptomatic of the slump. By 1981 the hotel had

seen eight different owners. The property's last use, before it was boarded up for 10 years, had been as a residential hotel.

In its early days the hotel had indeed been a gem, a manifestation of the enthusiasm San Jose's business leaders had for their developing downtown. The idea for the hotel came from a group of 27 prominent businessmen, who in 1929 formed the San Jose Community Hotel Company. The company proposed construction of a community-owned facility—it was "the distinctive, modern hotel in California"—that would capture the spirit and hospitality of downtown. The site, at what was then called West Santa Clara Street and Notre Dame Avenue, was selected because it afforded the

Luxurious without seeming overwhelming, Hotel DeAnza features such custom fixtures as etched-glass chandeliers, figured doors, and floral carpets.

The perfect place.

best view of the area and was accessible to the Southern Pacific train depot.

The hotel company hosted ground-breaking ceremonies in 1929, and opened the facility to guests a year later. A total of $505,000 was spent on construction of the hotel. The name was soon changed to Hotel DeAnza, which sounded more attractive to the hotel's stockholders and honored California explorer Juan Bautista de Anza.

As downtown business boomed, the hotel became a major focus of activity, attracting such guests as John F. Kennedy, Mickey Rooney, Olivia de Havilland, and Eleanor Roosevelt. The den-like El Capitan Bar, since replaced by The Hedley Club, earned a reputation as the place to meet. To the credit of its current owners and management team, this once-lost vibrancy is back. The rebirth of the DeAnza, an important and exciting part of the rebirth of downtown San Jose, is complete.

For the business traveler, Hotel DeAnza provides a working desk, multiple-line phone with voice mail message service, and a dedicated data line and FAX port, all in a spacious and comfortable room.

SAN MATEO COUNTY EXPO CENTER

The San Mateo County Expo Center evolved out of a desire to preserve a Bay Area tradition: the San Mateo County Fair and Floral Fiesta. First held in 1935, the Fair and Floral Fiesta was organized into an annual event starting in 1946, the same year San Mateo County officials formalized plans to accommodate the event with year-round exhibit facilities.

In 1948 the county completed the first of these facilities, the 50,000-square-foot Hall of Flowers, on 23 acres of land purchased from William Kyne, owner of neighboring Bay Meadows Race Track in San Mateo. Later renamed Fiesta Hall, this structure is one of seven fully equipped buildings now comprising Expo Center's 225,000 square feet of indoor exhibit space.

In addition to hosting a modern version of the annual Fair and Floral Fiesta, the Expo Center, which can accomodate 1,233 exhibit booths, is the forum for some of the region's most popular consumer and trade shows. Enthusiasm for these events is, in fact, very much in the spirit of that first county fair in 1935, which featured a parade, exhibits of rare birds and fish, and fireworks. In spite of rain on opening day, the fair attracted 60,000 visitors. Current attendance figures show that more than one million people visit the center annually, generating an estimated $50 million in sales for local businesses and services.

Improvements at the Expo Center, which now includes 48 acres of land, have been funded by contributions secured through the California Horse Racing Act and by Expo Center profits. And even though the Expo Center is now one of the busiest facilities of its kind in the Bay Area, the board of directors is studying alternative growth potential for the near future.

The Expo Center's affiliation with Fine Host Corporation has dramatically improved food services, including a freshly remodeled cafeteria. The center, in cooperation with Fine Host, also provides catered parties, seminars, and other events at the Expo Center. For information and a brochure, call (415) 574-3247, or (800) 338-EXPO outside California.

ABOVE: The forum for some of the region's most popular consumer and trade shows, the Expo Center can accommodate 1,233 exhibit booths.

LEFT: More than 750,000 people visit the San Mateo County Expo Center annually.

CASA MADRONA HOTEL AND RESTAURANT

William Barrett built it as his dream home in 1885. John Mays turned it into one of the Bay Area's finest vacation hotels 91 years later.

From the moment he saw Casa Madrona, Mays understood Barrett's dream. The Casa was more than a big hillside house with a view of Richardson Bay. It was a chunk of Sausalito history, a 20-room Victorian and Italianate testimonial to a more genteel time, a building that had survived the decades with dignity.

Barrett, a prosperous utility-industry official from San Francisco, kept the house until 1906, after which a succession of owners ran it as a residence hotel. In 1973, however, heavy rains and mudslides undermined Casa Madrona's foundation and put its future in jeopardy. Fortunately, Sausalito citizens rallied to preserve the house, raising almost $20,000 in donations for a temporary shoring-up of the foundation. In 1975 the city designated Casa Madrona a local landmark.

But the Casa's true salvation came a year later, when Mays, a litigation attorney with a San Francisco law firm, fell prey to its magic.

The driving sentiment behind Mays' purchase of Casa Madrona violated a cardinal rule of real estate investment: never fall in love with the property you buy. But it couldn't be helped. In spite of the building's structural problems and its extensive renovation needs, Mays was captivated by its charm, which still is Casa Madrona's most treasured asset.

Restoration commenced with painting and cleaning—but eventually progressed well beyond that. By 1984, after seemingly interminable wrangling between Mays and local antigrowth factions, the house's foundation had been retrofitted and 16 additional guest rooms covered the hillside, linking the main entry down on Bridgeway Street with the beautifully restored Casa up on the hill.

As improvements were made, little of Casa Madrona's romantic potential was lost on Mays, who had each of the hotel's 35 guest rooms designed and decorated with a separate theme. The old Casa, now called the Victorian House, offers options such as the Posada Room, with its canopy bed, redwood trim, and view of Sausalito Harbor, and the Belle Vista Suite, with its free-standing bathtub in the living room and view of the San Francisco skyline.

The New Casa—in which no two rooms have the same shape or atmosphere but all have a touch of the old Casa's romance—includes the Renoir Room, the Artist's Loft, and the Rose Chalet.

Casa Madrona Restaurant, also upgraded in the renovation, shares the dramatic view of San Francisco Bay and delights patrons with regional American dishes prepared with fresh ingredients and consummate skill. The restaurant's wine list, a perennial winner of the Wine Spectator's Award of Excellence, perfectly complements the ambience and food.

CALIFORNIA PARLOR CAR TOURS

California and the Pacific Northwest are home to some of the nation's best-known tourist resorts and national parks. California Parlor Car Tours covers the distances between these attractions, as well as uncertainties about hotel and restaurant accommodations, with a

combination of tour packages and bus travel that has been consistently popular since the company's founding in the 1920s.

The inspiration for this service came from rail-

partners purchased the company.

Bipin, a native of Uganda who started as a messenger boy with Greyhound in 1970, takes particular pride and care in maintaining the company's original mandate, which is to combine for customers the pleasures of guided sightseeing with the ease and comfort of the best motorcoach transportation available, hotel accommodations and meals included.

Unlike their rough-riding, noisy predecessors,

Current owners Ramesh Ramaiya, left, and his brother Bipin acquired California Parlor Car Tours in 1985.

California Parlor Car Tours' current fleet of sleek 40-foot 102 C3 motorcoaches is equipped with tinted windows, restrooms, reclining seats, and air conditioning.

road parlor cars, which provided some of the most luxurious travel available during the 1920s. R.C. Smith, a bus and truck salesman, and J.A. Boyd, a San Francisco guide, saw no reason bus interiors couldn't be equipped with parlor car amenities and used for tours on California's growing system of highways. In 1924, after modifying a small fleet of buses, Smith and Boyd started a company called Parlor Car Tours that featured three-day tours between San Francisco and Los Angeles.

The two men ran the company five years before selling it to Southern Pacific Motor Transport Company, which renamed it California Parlor Car Tours. In the late 1930s the business was acquired by Greyhound Lines, Inc., which kept it in operation—except for a hiatus during World War II—until 1985, when current owners Bipin Ramaiya, his brother Ramesh, and some

the company's current fleet of sleek 40-foot 102 C3 motorcoaches is equipped with tinted windows, restrooms, reclining seats, and air conditioning. Tour narration is provided by coach drivers, although the company gradually is adding separate managers to its tours to provide a better level of service. The company is also attentive to travel-industry trends and customers' comments, always ready to fine-tune its service.

And yet the basic service remains unchanged. While the quality and range of the company's tour-package offerings has improved beyond anything imagined by Boyd and Smith, their original notion of parlor-car bus service still succeeds intact. With a customer base that includes more than 60 percent of California's overnight bus tour market, California Parlor Car Tours is transforming a unique travel business into a tradition.

NOB HILL LAMBOURNE

As a businesswoman with international holdings, Barbara Brittingham shared the frustrations of those who do business on the road without easy access to fax machines, desktop computers and voice mail. And then Brittingham turned frustration into opportunity.

Opened in August 1989, the Nob Hill Lambourne provides traveling executives not only luxury accommodations but a full range of business-communications amenities in each room. In an era when catering to business travelers has become common at hotels of every persuasion, the catering often amounts to no more than a business center the size of a walk in closet. That is not the case at the 20-room Nob Hill Lambourne tucked away on a mostly residential street atop Nob Hill.

Billed as "a guest accommodation for the executive that doesn't want to get away from it all," The Nob Hill Lambourne has equipped every room and suite with an IBM PS/2 model 30-286 personal computer loaded with Lotus 1-2-3 and WordPerfect software, a Ricoh fax machine, and a telephone with two lines and voicemail. The hotel's Business Center augments these in-room resources with a Macintosh II/CX, Apple Laser Writer, Hewlett Packard Series II printer, two modems, and a photocopier.

The room decor is a blend of contemporary and period styles. Earthen colors were chosen to provide a feeling of warmth and to be conducive to a relaxed mood. The Nob Hill Lambourne has stayed away from a commercial hotel look and feel so you shouldn't be surprised by Proton AM-FM stereos, VCR's, and work stations complete with staplers and paper clips.

Buttressing these amenities is the kind of personalized service that only a small hotel can offer. The Nob Hill Lambourne is far from computer-driven; the detail oriented staff greets guests by name and provides quiet and efficient service. Questions about restaurants, entertainment, and recreational activities are fielded expertly by both the staff and a computer program that lists the locations and phone numbers of everything from the city's best restaurants to shopping and ATM banking services.

It is easy to see that catering to the needs to today's traveling executive has turned a new corner with the advent of The Nob Hill Lambourne.

THE SHOWPLACE SQUARE GROUP

When one visits the Galleria and Showplace Design Centers in San Francisco, it is hard to imagine their humble origins.

One-time warehouses in an aging area south of San Francisco's Market Street, the early-twentieth-century buildings attracted the attention of Henry Adams, who in the 1960s envisioned their potential as a wholesale home-furnishings complex.

Under Adams' supervision these brick buildings blossomed with new profiles and personalities, becoming the heart of a major West Coast design center called Showplace Square. These properties house approximately 3,000 manufacturers and 150 spectacular showrooms with top-name furnishings and accessories, from French antiques to fine fabrics.

Adams' first conversion, the four-story Dunham, Carrigan Hayden hardware supply warehouse on Kansas Street, became the 200,000-square-foot Showplace Design Center, a prime showcase for the residential interior design industry. The Design Center's penthouse offers magnificent views of San Francisco, a rooftop garden terrace, and complete facilities for private parties.

Across Kansas Street, later named Henry Adams Street by the City of San Francisco, Adams united two four-story brick warehouses with a spectacular glass and steel atrium court. He named the 200,000-square-foot structure the Galleria Design Center. The Galleria atrium, which has a retractable ceiling, is a prime location for social and business events.

Adams died in 1981 and in April 1983 San Francisco-based Bay West Development purchased the buildings. Bay West president Bill Poland and his partners, Kathleen Boarman, Trudy Drypolcher, and Tim Treadway, continued Adams' plan to create a major design center district.

In addition to the renovated Showplace and Galleria design centers, Bay West purchased another warehouse, which, with a 200,000-square-foot expansion, became the Contract Design Center, headquarters for business furniture in the Northern California.

These three design centers, plus the 132,000-square-foot Concourse Exhibition Center and the 25,000-square-foot Garden Court, comprise the Bay West-owned buildings now known as the Showplace Square Group. The Concourse Exhibition Center serves as a special event, consumer show, trade show, and exhibit facility. The Garden Court houses additional showrooms emphasizing both interior and exterior furnishings.

Apart from the success shared by the tenants

in these facilities, Showplace Square Group has rekindled interest in San Francisco's South of Market area, which now abounds with extensive building renovations and new construction.

LEFT: The 200,000-square-foot Galleria Design Center unites two four-story brick warehouses with a spectacular glass and steel atrium court.

BELOW: The Contract Design Center is headquarters for business furniture in Northern California.

NESTLE BEVERAGE COMPANY

RIGHT: The world's first vacuum-packed coffee was introduced by Hills Bros. in 1900. Vacuum packing led to the development of blends and enabled distant localities to receive fresh coffee. The gold miners of Alaska became familiar with the turbaned man on the red tapered can, because the vacuum-packed can gave them fresh coffee even in the frozen north. Hills Bros. still remains one of Alaska's favorite coffees.

BELOW: The Nestlé Beverage Company family of products.

Nestlé Beverage Company is the kind of Bay Area success story best told over a cup of Hills Bros. Coffee. In little more than 100 years, the company that started as a small, family-run business in San Francisco has become part of the largest food company in the world.

Nestlé Beverage Company was formed in March 1991 and is one of six divisions of Nestlé USA, a subsidiary of Swiss-based Nestlé S.A. Originally known as Hills Bros. Coffee, Inc., then briefly as Nestlé/Hills Bros. Coffee, Inc., the company has grown termendously since its inception in 1878 as a San Francisco-based dairy-products retailer.

In 1882 Austin and Rueben Hills purchased the Arabian Coffee & Spice Mills. By 1900 they were producing the best coffee on the West Coast. The Hills brothers were true innovators when it came to coffee, and invented techniques which were to become standards in the industry. One such technique, "cup testing," became the norm for judging the quality of coffee by tasting it "in the cup" as opposed to the accepted method of relying on the appearance of the beans. Another Hills Bros.-invented process was vacuum packing, which prevented coffee from oxidizing, thus losing freshness, once it was in the container. This innovation greatly extended the shelf life of the product and opened up new sales and distribution opportunities.

Hills Bros. Coffee, Inc., continued to expand

its sales and distribution throughout the 1900s. In 1984 the company was purchased by Nestlé S.A. That same year, Chase & Sanborn was acquired by Hill Bros., and a year later MJB was added to the company. As the gourmet coffee market continued to gain in popularity, Sark's Supreme Coffee Co. was purchased in 1987 and added to the Hills Bros. family of fine coffees.

More changes were in store for the landmark San Francisco company. In August 1990 Nestlé decided to consolidate its coffee operations, bringing its Taster's Choice and Nescafe brands, which had previously been produced and marketed by Nestlé Foods in Purchase, New York, to San Francisco to create one coffee company—Nestlé/Hills Bros. Coffee Co.

Just eight months later another consolidation brought all of the Nestlé beverages produced in the United States together to form one total beverage company. Thus Nestlé/Hills Bros. became Nestlé Beverage Company in March 1991. In addition to its already well-established coffee brands, the company also became responsible for Nestlé Quik, Nestea, Nestlé Hot Cocoa, Carnation Coffee-mate, Carnation Hot Cocoa, Carnation Malted Milk, and Libby's and Kern's juices and nectars.

A leader in the beverage industry, Nestlé Beverage Company employs more than 4,000 people and maintains 13 different manufacturing facilities throughout the country. The company's headquarters are still in San Francisco, located at 345 Spear Street in Hills Plaza along the Embarcadero.

Coffee taster Dub Hay at work.

Consolidated Freightways, Inc.

Back in 1929 Leland James, the son of a riverboat pilot, decided he could make a better living moving freight instead of people. With that idea, he sold his successful Portland, Oregon, bus line and opened a small trucking business called Consolidated Freight Lines.

James hoped that by providing good service at a fair price, he could build his new business venture into a modest success. He had an idea that he thought made sense, particularly since trucking was an industry in its infancy, yet to establish its future role as the backbone of American commerce.

ABOVE: Emery Worldwide is the largest carrier of heavy air freight in the United States.

BELOW: CF MotorFreight is a long-haul motor carrier for less-than-truckload freight shipments in North America.

That Depression-era gamble exceeded James' most optimistic expectations. Over the next 63 years, Consolidated Freightways drove the development of the modern motor carrier industry to become the biggest and perhaps most successful freight transportation company in the United States.

Today Consolidated Freightways, Inc. serves *Fortune* 500 companies and thousands of medium and small businesses. It has 12 different freight transportation entities that produce $4.1 billion in revenues, employ 37,000 people, operate 50,000 trucks, tractors, and trailers, and a fleet of aircraft that serve virtually every community through more than 1,300 freight terminals in North America.

Headquartered in the San Francisco Bay Area since 1956, the CF companies play a significant role in the daily ebb and flow of commerce that drives our nation's economy. Whether it's across town or across the country, a CF company can bring to bear cost-effective, high quality transportation services to meet any shipment need of business and industry.

Indeed, the company's only product is service. With today's focus on "just in time" and "quick response" production and retail inventory systems, freight transportation companies like CF have become a "warehouse on wheels" for commercial businesses and their customers. CF's services link suppliers, manufacturers, distribution centers, and retailers, bringing to market virtually every product or commodity we use in our daily lives.

The CF companies comprise three principal operating components:

• CF MotorFreight is a long-haul motor carrier for less-than-truckload freight shipments in the United States and Canada. As an "LTL" carrier, it specializes in moving commercial and industrial freight shipments from 10 to 10,000 pounds. Its nationwide Freight Flow System uti-

lizes 29 "consolidation centers" strategically located in a hub-and-spoke network across the U.S. to move shipments among thousands of destinations. The motor carrier has 675 terminals that cover more than 50,000 cities nationwide. The company's 20,000 employees handle about 55,000 freight shipments and serve some 300,000 customers each day.

• Con-Way Transportation Services provides regional trucking, intermodal full-truckload, and export ocean freight services. The Con-Way companies were formed in the early 1980s to take advantage of new markets that had emerged under deregulation of the trucking industry. They have grown from a start-up venture into the fastest growing regional trucking enterprise in the nation, with revenues approaching $700 million in 1992. Within CTS are four regional motor carriers specializing in next-day delivery, each serving a specific geographic area of the U.S. They are Con-Way Western Express, serving California, Arizona and Nevada; Con-Way Central Express, which operates in 11 Midwestern states; Con-Way Southern Express, serving nine southeastern states; and Con-Way Southwest Express, in Texas, Oklahoma, New Mexico, Louisiana, Arkansas, Mississippi, southern Alabama, and western Tennessee. The Con-Way regional carriers combined have 250 service centers and 7,000 employees. Con-Way Intermodal specializes in the movement of full-truckload shipments nationwide by rail piggyback, by container stack train, and through its premium Con-Quest Service; it also provides export ocean freight services with its innovative GLOBALRATE program.

• Emery Worldwide, a billion-dollar air freight company with 234 service locations in North America and 90 countries, is the largest carrier of commercial air freight in the U.S., with more than 25 percent of the market in North America for shipments above 70

pounds. It offers professional transportation services supporting the traffic and logistics needs of retailing, manufacturing, and industrial customers. Emery Worldwide's operations revolve around a state-of-the-art sortation hub in Dayton, Ohio, supported by an extensive ground network of trucks and terminals. With a fleet of dedicated aircraft and forwarding services, Emery moves all types of time-sensitive parcels, packages, and heavy freight shipments for same-day, next-day, second-day, or deferred delivery anywhere in the U.S. The company's international operations connect all major overseas trade points. Regular flights serve Europe, where shipments are routed through the company cargo hub in Brussels, Belgium, as well as Japan and Asia and the Pacific Rim. Emery provides extensive charter services and maintains an in-house customs brokerage service. The company's certificated airline affiliate, Emery Worldwide Airlines, operates planes for the airfreight operation and a dedicated fleet of 23 aircraft for the U.S. Postal Service to move Express and Priority Mail among 32 U.S. cities.

Consolidated Freightways, Inc. is publicly traded on the New York, London, and Pacific stock exchanges, and has been a member of the Dow Jones Industrial Average since 1970.

With truck fleet operations each year putting more than 800 million miles on America's highways, CF companies place considerable emphasis on safety. At CF MotorFreight, 34 of the company's drivers have attained 3 million miles without an accident—a milestone that took more than 30 years of professional driving to achieve. More than 2,500 drivers have reached the one-million-mile safe driving plateau. In 1991 CF MotorFreight and the Con-Way companies sent 56 drivers—one of the largest contingents from any one organization—to the National Truck Driving Championships. The event, held annually for more than 50 years, brings together more than 300 of the nation's best drivers (there are 6 million truck drivers in America) to face off in an annual safety and skills competition for the title of best truck driver in the U.S.

While the trucking industry thrives on moving freight, it could not survive without technology—and the CF companies are the industry's leaders. From the second a shipment is picked up to the second it is delivered, its progress is tracked and managed by the company's nationwide computer and telecommunications network. This on-line mainframe computer network processes more than 2 billion individual instructions per minute as some 100 million pounds of freight move among 1,300 terminals—all with pinpoint control.

The nationwide on-line computer network, laser bar-code scanning, computer aided dispatching, and on-board truck computers are all examples of a $300-million investment in technology the company has made in the past 10 years. CF also recently became the first in the industry to introduce optical laser-disk image processing. Trucking is paper-intensive business; CF daily generates 200,000 customer shipping documents alone. Over a year, those documents would create a stack 75 miles high. Today that stack has been reduced to electronic images, with 60,000 stored on a laser disk the size of a phonograph record. The system has dramatically improved productivity, cutting by two-thirds the 500,000 hours the company spends each year in manual document processing. Customer service has been improved as well; customers now can receive exact copies of shipping documents in one day via fax machine instead of the previous seven to ten days using manual methods. This allows CF's customers to speed their billing process, improving their cash flow and customer service.

With more than 6,000 freight transportation companies in the U.S., Consolidated Freightways, Inc. is in one of the most competitive and service-intensive industries in the country. It is also one of the most important to the well-being of the national economy. By combining a well-run business network with quality service, dedicated people, and the latest technology, Consolidated Freightways, Inc. is pushing its performance to the top of the transportation business.

ABOVE: Con-Way Transportation Services provides regional trucking, intermodal full-truck-load, and export ocean freight services.

BUSINESS

T he Bay Area's solid financial base has provided a dynamic environment for economic growth and opportunity for both individuals and businesses in the community.

▲ RE/MAX of California ▲ Hood and Strong ▲ Metropolitan Life Insurance Company ▲ Towers Perrin ▲ Cohn & Wells ▲ Thelen Marrin Johnson & Bridges ▲ American Express ▲ Aetna Life and Casualty ▲ Richard N. Goldman and Company

Photo by Ed Young/The Photo File

❏ ❏ ❏

RE/MAX OF CALIFORNIA

RIGHT: The famous RE/MAX balloon.

The name RE/MAX stands for "Real Estate Maximums." And it befits a company that, in less than 20 years, has gone from inception to the second-largest real estate franchise firm in all of North America. The remarkable story began in 1973, when a Denver real estate agent opened his own office based on a concept of paying agents 100 percent of the standard commission.

The RE/MAX concept is similar to that of a cooperative. Sales agents retain all of the standard commission on properties they sell, paying the Broker/Owner a monthly fee to cover the agent's proportionate share of the expenses. The 100 percent of the commission concept, compared to the 50/50 or 60/40 split in traditional real estate offices, has attracted thousands of top producers in the industry.

The result is that RE/MAX agents have an average of 9.5 years of experience, compared with an industry average of 4 years, and earn 3.5 times as much as the average agent. They also handle about 60 percent more transactions annually than their counterparts in traditional offices.

Nowhere has the growth of RE/MAX been more dramatic than in California, due to the efforts of two men who had already built an extremely successful real estate sales organization of their own. By 1982 Spring Realty, under the leadership of Sid Syvertson and Steve Haselton, had grown with quality, dignity, and pride to become one of the 10 largest privately held real estate firms in the United States, with some 30 offices and 1,000 sales agents in Southern California. The firm was founded in 1962 by Syvertson, and Haselton became his partner in 1968.

As successful as they had grown, both men realized they were a long way from their common goal of becoming a significant factor in California real estate. While considering various traditional ways to expand their operation, they were convinced that, whatever their decision was to be, it required an idea that was revolutionary, not evolutionary. They studied the RE/MAX concept carefully and decided it met their requirements by offering the best opportunity for achieving their long-term objectives.

On August 30, 1982, RE/MAX of California was launched, with all Spring Realty offices shifting to the new operation in a transition that was to be the largest conversion in the history of RE/MAX. Managers of the old offices became owners and franchisees under the California master franchise owned by Syvertson and Haselton.

In the hands of the two men, the RE/MAX concept has given a new dimension to real estate in California. RE/MAX of California had grown to more than 200 offices and 3,000 agents by the end of the 1980s. In 1989 alone its agents closed 41,000 transactions representing nearly $10 billion in sales, making it the largest RE/MAX region in the United States. It reached that lofty position after just seven years within the RE/MAX network.

RE/MAX of California's more than 3,500 agents are always "top of mind" for Syvertson and Haselton. Since these agents form the basis of the region's remarkable success, the two men view their main task as seeing that the agents have the support they need.

The support mechanisms the pair have devised during their seven-year RE/MAX

Sid Syvertson (standing) and Steve Haselton, co-owners of RE/MAX of California

The *Spruce Goose* was
the site of the 1992
RE/MAX Annual Awards
Banquet.

alliance ranges from choosing Broker/Owners who can recruit the best agents in the first place to aiding these brokers in creating work environments attractive to California's best real estate sales agents. Office design, communications, advertising, and awards ceremonies also play major parts in the regional programs. In every area, function takes precedence over cosmetic concerns.

Syvertson and Haselton's philosophy for success is practical rather than theoretical: Find out what agents and owners want and make it easy for them to get it. One of the first factors in keeping agents productive and happy, the two men believe, lies in selecting Broker/Owners who understand the RE/MAX concept and its potential. Great care and emphasis is placed on the selection of new franchisees to assure the people selected can recruit the caliber of professionals needed to build an office of top producers. People who can build their own dreams as well as those of RE/MAX of California.

Syvertson and Haselton feel the region's success can also be attributed to support programs like communications and advertising as exemplified by the award-winning *RE/MAX in California* regional magazine, the advertising program, and the annual convention and awards banquet.

Both men stress it is important to remind agents of the revolutionary nature of the RE/MAX organization, and the magazine is designed to convey this message. The regional advertising program is also multipurpose. In the mediums of television, radio, and print, the current slogan "RE/MAX—The Maximum Real Estate Has To Offer" is used.

RE/MAX of California agents like to celebrate their success together. To provide a gala ocassion for the celebration, Haselton and Syvertson produce an annual awards weekend that is a production of staging, lighting, sound, and educational events.

Sid Syvertson and Steve Haselton are justifiably proud of their success but, in typical fashion, have set much higher goals for themselves and their company. Determined to be the largest real estate firm in a state where the population increases by 600,000 annually, they plan to have 400 offices and 6,800 agents throughout California by the mid-1990s.

Never failing to recognize and seize opportunities to build their organization, the two men decided a few years ago to expand from a strictly residential operation into commercial real estate sales as well. Several offices in California, using the same 100 percent concept, have been opened and now account for about 20 percent of the firm's business.

The story of RE/MAX of California is a classic example of the principle of synergism, elements that combine to produce a total effect that is greater than the sum of the individual elements. The combining of an already very successful real estate firm with the "revolutionary" RE/MAX network system is an excellent example of synergism. An even better example is the combination of Sid Syvertson and Steve Haselton, two very successful but very different men who, in joining forces, have produced a total effect that not only is greater than the sum of their individual accomplishments but at the same time has made real estate history in California.

HOOD AND STRONG

Hood and Strong, one of the oldest and largest independent CPA firms in Northern California, has prospered by guiding Bay Area businesses to sound financial management and a prosperity of their own.

Founded in 1917, Hood and Strong built its success on traditional audit and tax services. To meet the needs of its clients, the firm has expanded its services to include management advisory, integrated business, employee benefits, and information services. Perhaps more importantly, it has based its practice on a personalized approach to delivering its services. Through the years, Hood and Strong has focused primarily on assisting middle-market family businesses and closely held service companies—businesses not unlike Hood and Strong itself. Some of its clients have worked with the firm since its inception; others are newcomers and start-up companies. All of them have Bay Area roots.

Hood and Strong's more than 100 professional accountants and support staff are managed by 20 partners. Both partners and accountants work directly with clients, customizing services to each client's needs. "A lot of what we do," says Hood and Strong partner Mollie Marshall, "is consult with clients to help them achieve their specific company goals."

The firm's audit, accounting, and management-consulting specialists ensure that those client goals are met. The firm is skilled at matching its specialists with the specific technical needs of each client. As part of its client-service philosophy, Hood and Strong combines departmentalized technical services with creative and personalized services to achieve maximum efficiency and cost/benefit advantages.

Hood and Strong's audit services are supplemented by a range of financial and strategic

consulting programs. The firm's tax services, meanwhile, emphasize tax planning for corporations, partnerships, and individuals. There is a close link between the tax planning for the corporation and the related owners. The employee benefits consulting department works with companies to ensure that they are maximizing their employee benefits programs.

Hood and Strong's management advisory services include management information system design and implementation, systems evaluation, operations reviews, and continuous process quality improvement programs. For smaller clients, the firm's integrated business services (IBS) department offers a year-round program of consultation, financial statement preparation and evaluation, tax planning, and general business

consulting. If the company is too small to invest in a full-time chief financial officer, but big enough to require the business and financial savvy a CFO provides, then Hood and Strong's IBS department is the solution.

The sixth Hood and Strong department, information services, offers services under the name of DATAFIND. This service retrieves and organizes information on numerous business and industry topics for use by both clients and staff.

The firm's newest department, litigation support, combines technical accounting experience with detailed anaysis to provide attorneys and their clients with a wide range of services.

In targeting family-owned and closely held businesses, Hood and Strong has tapped into the Bay Area's broadest market. Wholesale distributors, mortgage bankers, real estate managers, contractors, nonprofit organizations, and wealthy individuals dominate Hood and Strong's client list. Hood and Strong has become the leader in the Bay Area in the wholesale distribution industry. The firm conducted the first Bay Area management and performance survey of more than 1,800 distributors in the Bay Area. With its specialized services, Hood and Strong assists distributors in profitability analysis, continuous process improvement, and financial management. Hood and Strong is also a leader in the mortagage banking industry. Mortgage bankers throughout California utilize the firm's services in this specialized industry.

Hood and Strong's ability to deliver outstanding service to these clients is augmented by its active participation in professional associations through memberships on both national and state-wide committees.

Hood and Strong is a member of the Private Company Practice Section and the SEC Practice Section of the Division of CPA firms. Both organizations participate in regular peer reviews, in which independent teams of CPAs examine

ABOVE: A Hood and Strong audit team plans a site inspection.

member firms' systems of quality control for accounting and auditing services. In each of its peer reviews, Hood and Strong has received an unqualified opinion on its system of quality-control and related procedures.

Another key to the uniformly high quality of Hood and Strong's work, particularly for clients with multi-state and international operations, is its affiliation with Associated Accounting Firms International (AAFI) and Summit International Associates, Inc.

AAFI is a national association of about 35 independent CPA firms that share expertise, technical and management information, training programs, and other resources. Summit International, which includes more than 60 independent accounting firms in 40 countries, provides its members' clients with a global network of CPA resources.

In addition to maintaining its standard of excellent work, Hood and Strong will face the future with at least one other constant—growth. As the Bay Area grows, so will Hood and Strong, enhancing its ability to serve clients throughout the region. "We will continue to look at acquisition opportunities," says Robert Docili, managing partner, "in order to provide better client service and opportunities for our partners and staff. We're looking at ourselves to be the primary local CPA firm in the Bay Area."

LEFT: Hood and Strong's clients have operations throughout the United States.

METROPOLITAN LIFE INSURANCE COMPANY

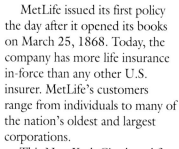

A major and longtime presence in the Bay Area, MetLife is one of the largest financial institutions in the world. The company and its affiliates have more than $130 billion of assets under management and provide or administer coverage to more than 45 million people in the United States, Canada, Europe, and the Far East.

MetLife offers one of the most diverse and competitive portfolios of insurance and financial products available to Bay Area residents and businesses. These products are backed by excellent service, MetLife's financial stability, and its continued commitment to core businesses— group insurance, personal insurance, pensions, and investments.

Another MetLife hallmark is a long tradition of corporate citizenship and community involvement. Ten days after the Loma Prieta earthquake struck the Bay Area in October 1989, MetLife announced a grant of $100,000 to support the American Red Cross Disaster Relief Fund. The company's AIDS education activities—part of its overall commitment to health and safety education—have helped support local programs such as the San Francisco AIDS Foundation. MetLife is also a major corporate sponsor of the San Francisco Ballet.

Going back in time, to the earthquake of 1906, MetLife was the first to send a special team into the city to pay claims on the spot.

MetLife issued its first policy the day after it opened its books on March 25, 1868. Today, the company has more life insurance in-force than any other U.S. insurer. MetLife's customers range from individuals to many of the nation's oldest and largest corporations.

This New York City-based firm also has made innovation a watchword. It was the first insurance company to issue policies to substandard risks—previously uninsurable people who could not get coverage elsewhere. And it was the first insurer to extend group insurance into the pension field for retired employees.

More recently, MetLife has done pioneering work with group insurance programs such as vision care, dental care, pension and profit-sharing plans, and flexible benefits plans that allow employees to select benefits.

MetLife opened its San Francisco office in 1901, the Pacific Coast Head Office, to establish closer contact with its West Coast policyholders. Today, MetLife's Western Group Operations are located in downtown San Francisco, and its Personal Insurance operations are headquartered in San Ramon.

MetLife currently employs more than 1,000 Bay Area residents, has $56 billion of insurance in force in California, and boasts a local client base that includes Chevron, Bechtel Power Corporation, Pacific Gas & Electric, Kaiser Aluminum & Chemical, and the Bank of California.

Statewide, MetLife has provided one billion dollars in residential and commercial loans and has another $900 million in other real estate investments in the Bay Area, including 50 California Street in San Francisco and River Park Towers and the Technology Center in San Jose.

Looking ahead, MetLife and its competitors face special challenges in the area of health care given the West Coast's political and consumer climate. "MetLife's long-term approach," says Joseph W. Mullen, Jr., vice-president of Western Group Insurance Operations, "is to forge partnerships with health care providers and customers to give customers and their employees access to quality care at an affordable cost."

The company is now looking at revised group insurance programs in which employees could choose from a variety of flexible coverage plans and compensate the insurer through payroll deductions. "Employers want to provide a benefits program at a reasonable cost," says Mullen. "MetLife would be able come in and offer a complete range of products, such as life, auto, and homeowners insurance. The workplace would become the distribution system."

Bringing such suggestions into practice, Mullen adds, requires a market, such as the Bay Area, that accepts innovation. "Many people in the Bay Area—lawyers, labor, community groups, and providers of health care—have expressed an interest in innovation and in sitting down to work on solutions," he says. "This is a healthy sign."

ABOVE: MetLife's Western Group Operations is headquartered in this modern office building at the corner of Market and Fremont streets in San Francisco.

LEFT: As this photograph shows, MetLife has conducted business in San Francisco for nearly a century.

TOWERS PERRIN

I n 1917, an ancestor organization of what would become Towers, Perrin, Forster & Crosby (TPF&C) designed one of the first private pension plans in the United States. Today, Towers Perrin is one of the nation's leading management consulting companies, as well as one of the Bay Area's most important business consulting resources.

As of January 1, 1992, TPF&C and Cresap are combined under the name of Towers Perrin. Along with partner company Tillinghast — an insurance and risk management consulting firm — Towers Perrin provides a comprehensive range of management consulting services that is internationally recognized for finding solutions

tion practices were formally established in 1934 as Towers, Perrin, Forster & Crosby, originally located in Philadelphia. The San Francisco office opened in 1959.

Cresap, McCormick & Paget, established in 1946, became the general management consulting division of Towers Perrin in 1983. Cresap's consultants work with senior managers of client firms to help them achieve maximum return from strategic, marketing, organizational, and operational components of their businesses. Cresap's general services are also supported by specialists in information systems, public utilities, energy, financial institutions, and the transportation industry.

Towers Perrin employees from the three operating units meet to discuss the current market trends in management consulting.

to business problems. More than 10,000 corporate and institutional clients worldwide — including 95 percent of the *Fortune* 100 and 80 percent of the *Fortune* 500 industrial corporations — currently use Towers Perrin services. The firm's client list includes more than 80 percent of the largest American and Canadian industrial companies, plus a significant number of major national and multinational private and government-owned enterprises in Australia, Europe, and Asia. Many of these companies have been using Towers Perrin's services for more than three decades.

Following that initial pension plan assignment in 1917, the benefits and compensa-

Tillinghast, which joined Towers Perrin in 1986, is an international organization that has been providing actuarial and management advice to insurance companies — in life, health, and property/casualty — and related industries for more than 40 years. Formerly known as Tillinghast, Nelson and Warren, this company also delivers risk management services to businesses, nonprofit organizations, and government agencies.

A third division, Towers Perrin Reinsurance, is one of the major reinsurance intermediaries in the United States; it provides international service to the country's insurance industry.

With more than 5,000 employees — 650 of whom share ownership in the firm as partners — Towers Perrin is ranked as one of the world's largest privately held management consulting firms. The broad range of human resource and organizational capabilities, along with a commitment to provide the highest quality service, have attracted clients to Towers Perrin offices throughout Asia, Australia, Canada, Europe, Latin America, and the United States.

The San Francisco office was the company's first West Coast branch. More than 100 of the firm's clients are Bay Area companies working directly with San Francisco office personnel, but also benefiting from the firm's international network of consulting services. Towers Perrin provides expertise in all aspects of human resource and organization management — from actuarial calculations to benefits planning to compensation programs to strategic organizational planning. Although many of its clients are large firms, the consulting and client base in this office fully reflects the entrepreneurial spirit that attracts so many start-up ventures and service companies to the Bay Area.

In addition to Towers Perrin's cost-effective, objective, and fully independent counsel, clients benefit from the firm's impressive array of supplemental resources, including a confidential, client-centered database — accessible from any of Towers Perrin's 61 offices worldwide — and the firm's large research, information, and technology staff, which produces studies of economic trends, business development, and human resource practices.

One such study, "Workforce 2000: Competing in a Seller's Market" (produced in conjunction with the Hudson Institute), showed that, while most American companies are concerned about the radical work force shifts predicted over the next decade, the extent to which they have taken specific actions in response varies widely. Coming demographic and cultural changes foretell labor and skills shortages in the available workers' pool at a time when the demand for both will increase. Additionally, companies that wish to compete will have to manage a work force that not only contains more women and minorities, but also is aging. This work force may be more dependent on the contributions of workers who are approaching or past retirement age. This study — the long-range problems it identifies and the solutions they require — has proven timely for many businesses in growing global markets such as the Bay Area.

One of Towers Perrin's primary long-term goals is to continue development of the programs and tools the country's and the region's businesses will need to respond to challenges such as "Workforce 2000" as we move into the next century. To that end, the San Francisco office — always at the forefront of the firm's consulting initiatives — has set the highest standards for putting those initiatives into practice and meeting the unique demands of Bay Area businesses.

COHN & WELLS

Martin Cohn and Bradley Wells

What do two ex-New York advertising men do when they come to San Francisco? Open up their own agency, of course.

It didn't happen right away. In fact, Martin Cohn and Bradley Wells were just passing acquaintances when they ran into each other in San Francisco in the early 1980s. Cohn had come to San Francisco to open Ogilvy & Mather Direct. Wells had relocated here to join another San Francisco agency.

Neither dreamed that in a couple of years they would team up to open Cohn & Wells, now the largest direct response agency on the West Coast.

It all happened almost as a series of accidents. Cohn, a copywriter/creative director for 12 years, left Ogilvy & Mather to pursue a freelance writing career. Wells, who had 15 years experience in account management in general advertising, decided it was time to start his own marketing consultancy.

Being colleagues and fellow ex-New Yorkers, the two had kept in touch. So when Bank of America proposed some projects that called for both creative direction and account management, it seemed only natural for Cohn and Wells to collaborate.

And when a couple of projects turned into ongoing work, the word "agency" began to surface. The big decision—whose name would come first—was solved alphabetically. Cohn & Wells was born.

Right from the start, Martin Cohn and Bradley Wells decided they would take a hands-on approach to handling their clients' projects. Using all of the strategies and techniques they had learned in their combined 27 years of experience, they personally developed every advertising program their clients needed. To this day, both Cohn and Wells are involved with every campaign that comes out of the agency.

In the beginning, there was Cohn, Wells, and a receptionist in a small downtown office. One of the things they always insisted on was a warm, friendly, charming atmosphere, so their first office was located in an old Victorian building on Mason Street. A visitor walking in to the original Cohn & Wells location would be met with marble fireplaces, antique furniture, and fresh flowers everywhere.

There was a steady flow of projects from Bank of America, Pacific Bell, and Gump's. Although Cohn & Wells' success came as something of a welcome surprise to its founders, in retrospect their formula for attracting business seemed guaranteed to work. "We wanted people's business more than anybody else did," Wells said, "So we just went in and asked for it. And, unlike New York, here in San Francisco people were willing to take risks in the hopes of hitting a home run."

Cohn & Wells hit many home runs. In fact, by the second year of the agency's existence, it stood unbeaten in every head-to-head test of response rates against every other agency their clients had used. The Cohn & Wells philosophy of providing the absolute best creative with unsurpassable service was paying off.

Not surprisingly, Cohn & Wells began to win more and more projects from existing clients. Later, more accounts came in from such blue-chip companies as Borland, Chevron, and PG&E.

By 1988 Cohn & Wells had outgrown its original

In 1988 Cohn & Wells moved to 451 Pacific Avenue, a remodeled firehouse that is a San Francisco landmark.

office. After a six-month search for a place that "doesn't look like a typical office," a suitable building was finally located—one of the oldest existing firehouses in San Francisco, Engine Company #1 at 451 Pacific Ave. This landmark building, built during the late nineteenth century, has undergone extensive interior remodeling but still retains the old brass pole and the drying racks for the fire hoses.

Cohn & Wells was growing so fast at the time of the move that a few months later the company had to lease space in two additional buildings down the street. "I knew we were getting pretty big when I couldn't find anybody to hire," Wells says, referring to the fact that he soon found himself shopping for talent outside San Francisco. The two partners still express amazement that the San Francisco office has grown to more than 50 people, with 20 more staffers divided between offices in Los Angeles, Chicago, and New York.

"The goal was to create an agency that was fun to work in, the kind of place we wanted to come to work at, compared with the typical agency," Cohn says. "We were hoping it might be six or eight people."

Along with growth have come some surprises. Such as being purchased by Euro-RSCG, a Paris-based advertising company, ranked as the number one ad network in Europe and number six worldwide.

The sale helped to expand Cohn & Wells' resources while allowing the agency to continue to function autonomously. In fact, on the home front Cohn & Wells has added three subsidiaries: MarketSmart, which specializes in database management; ACQ, which helps merging companies communicate quickly with newly acquired customers; and DMZ, a graphic design group that uses leading edge computer technology.

With the largest market share on the West Coast, Cohn & Wells has yet more plans for future expansion. The Los Angeles, Chicago, and New York offices are but the first manifestations of what will eventually be an international network of direct response agencies. Europe and Asia, watch out—the Madison Avenue of direct response agencies is on its way.

THELEN MARRIN JOHNSON & BRIDGES

Thelen, Marrin, Johnson & Bridges is one of the 10 largest and most successful law firms in California. Its business practice has dramatically expanded nationally and internationally since 1980, and the firm has more than doubled in size since 1984, with more than 300 attorneys operating in seven offices throughout the United States and one office in Hong Kong.

This rapid growth, however, is hardly the principal measure of the San Francisco-based firm's stature as a nationwide law practice.

Thelen, Marrin's partners have used expansion as an opportunity to enhance delivery of the firm's high-quality legal services. In a restructuring that began in 1990, the firm reduced the geographic autonomy of its offices and established management groups for each of its 10 practice specialties. With the support of a fully integrated computer system that electronically links every attorney and staff person, the attorneys in each specialty, no matter which office they work from, now have instant access to firmwide resources as well as greater cooperation and efficiency in using those resources.

Remarkably, this organizational realignment preserved the firm's inner strengths, creatively merging Thelen, Marrin's collegial traditions with contemporary concepts of management, and combining its commitment to social responsibility with practical leadership. Most important, the new structure increased productivity while it created a new sense of unity and a dynamic national presence—and the foundation for a multinational practice.

"Our partners want to position Thelen to serve the needs of multinational clients throughout the United States, Europe, and East Asia," says chairman Philip R. Placier, noting that Thelen, Marrin is among the first law firms in the country to implement such a structure. "The increasing globalization of our practice is our vision of the 1990s."

Thelen, Marrin's rise to competitiveness began in the 1920s, when it earned the trust of clients such as Warren A. Bechtel, founder of the Bechtel group of engineering and construction companies, and Henry J. Kaiser, founder of the Kaiser industrial empire.

Founded in 1924 by Max Thelen and Paul Marrin, the firm initially focused on the needs of clients involved in the financing, design, and construction or large projects. It represented Six Companies, the corporation formed for construction of the Hoover Dam, and was involved in the construction of the Golden Gate and Bay bridges. In 1942 such work prompted the opening of Thelen, Marrin's Los Angeles office, one of the first Los Angeles branch offices established by a Bay Area law firm.

After World War II, Thelen, Marrin's growing client base and range of expertise steadily broadened to include its 10 current practice specialties: antitrust, bankruptcy, business litigation, commercial finance, construction, corporate, labor and employment, real estate, tax and torts, insurance, and environmental.

In addition to Bechtel and Kaiser Aluminum & Chemical Corp., Thelen, Marrin's diverse list of clients now includes organizations such as Bank of America, Westinghouse Electric, the City of Santa Clara, Data General Corp., Dillingham Construction, Homestake Mining, Georgia Pacific, Louisiana Pacific, NEC Electronics and the San Francisco Newspaper Agency. The list continues to grow, and Thelen, Marrin with it.

The opening of the Hong Kong office in

1988, prompted by an increase in Pacific Rim work, was accompanied by the firm's participation in Interjura Consultancy, a consortium of international law firms established in Beijing in 1987 to service business clients in Beijing, P.R.C. And in 1990 Thelen, Marrin established a presence for service to clients in Europe through an alliance with the London-based law firm Turner, Kenneth, Brown.

What hasn't changed about the firm during its exceptional development is its commitment to community service. Within days after the October 1989, earthquake, for example, Thelen, Marrin donated $75,000, originally earmarked for year-end celebrations, to disaster relief. And the firm was among the first to provide pro bono legal services—a significant part of the firm's public-service program—to people returning from duty in the Persian Gulf and victims of the Oakland fire of October 1991.

The firm's contributions to the local community and its emergence on the international scene also illustrate an important point: No matter whom Thelen, Marrin serves—be it a pro bono recipient, a small business or a multinational Fortune 500 company—the quality of its legal work will always be up to its long-established standards of excellence. For Thelen, Marrin, Johnson & Bridges is committed to honoring the past, competing in the present and preparing for the future.

LEFT: A practice group structure joins attorneys firmwide in service of clients. Wayne Kirk (left), of the San Francisco office, and David Graybeal (of New York) are pictured in the firm's San Francisco office.

Thelen Marrin Johnson & Bridges is a leader in the use of technology to serve clients. All attorneys and staff have computer work stations, each electronically linked from London to Hong Kong.

AMERICAN EXPRESS

American Express was forged in 1850 from three express companies that transported gold and other valuables for customers. It has evolved over the years into today's diversified travel-related and financial services company, with over 100,000 employees and operations in over 120 countries worldwide. From its earliest days, the company developed and delivered products and services designed to provide security, convenience, and a sense of confidence to its customers.

Today, American Express consists of five separate businesses. The company's core business is operated by American Express Travel Related Services Company, Inc. (TRS), which has created and marketed some of the world's most distinctive and well-known brand names. These include the American Express® Card, the American Express® Travelers Cheque, and American

personal money management for nearly 100 years. Acquired in 1984, it serves the growing demand of more than one million American families for financial planning and investment services.

The fifth and newest American Express business, American Express Information Services Corporation, provides a variety of information processing, communication, and funds management services, including transaction processing for credit and debit cards.

Travel Related Services, or TRS, is the travel and life-style branch of American Express. Often described as the "heart and soul" of the company, it is a major Bay Area presence. In addition to its regional offices in San Francisco, TRS has several other Bay Area locations, making the full range of its travel related products and services available throughout the area. TRS,

Express® Travel Services. Other important TRS products and services are provided by such diverse business units as consumer lending, insurance, merchandise, and publishing.

The company's second-oldest business is American Express Bank Ltd., which was established in 1919. The bank's worldwide network of offices outside the United States offers commercial and personal financial services to meet the global needs of successful individuals.

In 1981 American Express acquired the securities and investment banking business of Shearson Loeb Rhodes, now known as Shearson Lehman Brothers Inc. Shearson is a leading full-line securities firm serving the financial needs of clients in the United States and in all of the major financial centers throughout the world.

IDS Financial Services Inc., the fourth major American Express business, has been a leader in

through its Travel Management Services (TMS) unit, serves the needs of everything from small businesses to *Fortune* 500 companies to public sector organizations, including government entities.

In fact, the State of California has chosen the American Express ®Corporate Card for the state's network of agencies—about 60,000 employees in all. In addition, American Express has travel management programs with hundreds of Bay Area businesses, assisting them in managing and controlling their business travel and entertainment expenses.

American Express' tradition of innovation began with Henry Wells. He established the forerunner of the American Express Company in 1841 when he safely carried a carpetbag full of gold, silver, and securities from Albany, New York, to his hometown of Buffalo. The four-day journey heralded the birth of Wells & Co., which in 1850 merged with two competitors, Butterfield, Wasson & Co. and Livingston & Fargo, to form the American Express Company.

As president of American Express, Wells was constantly searching for ways to improve and expand service, an approach very much in evidence at American Express today. Although American Express directors voted against the idea, Wells and company vice president William Fargo decided to capitalize on the express trade blossoming in the west, where gold had been discovered. In 1852 the two men formed Wells, Fargo and Company. A few years later, partner John Butterfield established another express operation, the Overland Mail, which featured the famed Pony Express.

By 1866, competition among express-service firms prompted a merger of American Express and Merchants Union Express Company, further expanding American Express' client base. By the turn of the century the company had introduced the American Express Money Order and its famous American Express Travelers Cheque, and had reorganized and increased its transatlantic freight business.

American Express began its first foray into the travel business in 1909, when it became a selling agent for European railroads and westbound transatlantic passenger vessels. In 1915 the company formally established its travel department in New York; it has become one of the world's most successful travel-related service operations.

American Express Travel was in fact one of a handful of the company's private enterprises that survived the government's 1918 consolidation of all railroad and express companies. Deprived of its express operations, the company's principals established in 1919 a subsidiary firm, the American Express Company, Incorporated, to further international expansion and to manage

travel, money orders, Travelers Cheques, foreign remittance, and foreign exchange, as well as the corporation's international freight business.

With the firm's growth in travel and travel-related services during the 1950s and 1960s—including the introduction of the American Express Card in 1958 and its servicing of the travel boom during the 1960s—American Express Travelers Cheques, the Card, and the company logo became the ubiquitous symbols of first-rate travel and financial services.

Throughout its history, American Express has built a reputation for integrity, quality, reliability, and extraordinary customer care. The company has repeatedly helped people in trouble when no one else could. During two World Wars, American Express rescued stranded travelers in Europe. In 1933, when the U.S. government declared a bank "holiday" and closed banks, American Express remained open and continued to cash its Travelers Cheques and honor American Express Money Orders. In 1975 the company provided military banking services in combat zones during the fall of Saigon. After the 1985 Mexico City earthquake, American Express employees set up an emergency travel office in the middle of a downtown street to serve travelers as well as local customers. In the spring of 1989 company employees came to the rescue of travelers caught up in the civil disturbances in Beijing. Feats such as these have become part of American Express history and help explain the company's deep commitment to quality service.

ABOVE: The reception area of the TRS regional headquarters, located at 525 Market Street.

The Post Street Travel Service office, located at Union Square.

AETNA LIFE AND CASUALTY

Provider of a vast array of insurance and financial products, Aetna Life and Casualty is the seventh-largest insurance company in the world and one of the most prominent in California.

The extent of Aetna's California operations, which include an office in Walnut Creek, is indicative not only of the care with which the company develops and refines its products but of its adaptability to an ever-changing market. California is, after all, at the forefront of regulatory and consumer trends.

And Aetna is at the forefront in tracking, analyzing, and responding to these trends, particularly as they affect automobile insurance, workers compensation, and employer liability protection. In addition, Aetna has kept pace with dramatic changes in the health care industry by fashioning a refurbished range of direct insurance products as well as managed-care services, health-maintenance organizations, and preferred-provider organizations.

These managed-care programs, which augment traditional indemnity products, give employees more choice in selecting coverages and give employers and clients the tools and incentives to control costs. The notion of customer choice, observes Alison G. Coolbrith, Aetna's vice president in Walnut Creek, has become one of the most compelling aspects for insurance companies such as Aetna to broaden their roles beyond traditional insurance mechanisms.

This consumer-oriented attitude also applies to the company's approach to handling claims. Among the many Aetna clients who suffered property damage because of the Loma Prieta earthquake in 1989, notes Coolbrith, several mistakenly failed to purchase coverage for certain affected properties. Nevertheless, these clients were compensated by Aetna in spite of the oversight.

Another way Aetna has cultivated success is through internal change and innovation, which enhance the company's ability to meet clients' needs precisely and at low cost. Some of the most sweeping changes involved a reorganization

Alison G. Coolbrith, vice-president. Photo by E. Carl Cierpial

in 1991-1993, which sharpened Aetna's focus on its best-performing services and products and streamlined company operations through innovative new technologies.

Aetna's San Francisco, California, office, for example, has pioneered the use of laptop computers, linked to the company's Commercial Processing System, in writing insurance coverage for selected small-business accounts. A computer link to the company's country-wide system has also helped Aetna operate its commercial-accounts offices with a high degree of efficiency. And thanks to its sensitivity to community and regional needs, Aetna's California offices, including its Bay Area offices, write more insurance for licensed day care PACE members than any other insurer in the state.

Founded in 1817 as the Aetna Insurance Company, the company's original charter was solely for fire insurance. The first incarnation of today's Aetna Life and Casualty, however, was established in 1853 by Hartford, Connecticut, attorney Eliphalet A. Bulkeley as the Aetna Life Insurance Company.

By 1907 the company had expanded its product line to include accident, health, and automobile insurance, and had established its first affiliate, the Aetna Accident and Liability Company. Aetna offered the first comprehensive auto insurance policy in 1912, developed several new types of coverage during World War II (including employee group insurance), and was first listed on the New York Stock Exchange in 1968.

The company's West Coast office opened in San Francisco in 1867 and served as a foundation for a statewide operation that now includes more than 2,700 employees and $5.2 billion in invested assets.

As it entered 1992, Aetna had more than $90 billion in company-wide assets and diversified portfolios in each of six divisions: health and life insurance, financial services, property and casualty insurance, reinsurance, and international operations.

Is there more room for innovation? Coolbrith believes there has to be. She says, "The companies that will prosper—and one will be Aetna—are the ones that are going to be adaptable, the ones that are very clear about why insurance costs what it does and what insurers and their agents should be delivering to the public, the people who allow us to operate profitably."

Golden Gate Bridge.
Photo by E. Carl Cierpial

RICHARD N. GOLDMAN AND CO.

When Richard Goldman started his own insurance brokerage in the mid-1950s, he knew that honesty, directness, and competitive ingenuity would guide his business to success. Today, Goldman Insurance is the leading and most respected insurance brokerage in Northern California.

This San Francisco-based firm offers the full spectrum of risk-management services, offering property/casualty, employee benefits, workers' compensation (the firm operates a seperate workers' compensation department), life, and personal lines coverages. Goldman's staff of more than 70 insurance professionals handles approximately $85 million in premiums annually, and sets itself apart with services not typically found at other brokerages, including 24-hour claims service and critical-loss mitigation through prompt, on-site response by its claims representatives.

With a client base of more than 500 companies, Goldman represents a broad range of concerns in the Bay Area and beyond. The firm boasts particular expertise in property-related fields, including development, property management, and real estate financing. Goldman also serves a host of prominent, nationally-based hotels and restaurants, professional service firms, larger manufacturers, retailers, and sports teams. Goldman's genuine commitment to the Bay Area community is further evidenced by its servicing and support of many nonprofilt organizations.

Richard Goldman and his wife, Rhoda, make community service a vital part of the firm's identity, and in 1989 established a trust fund to support the Goldman Environmental Prize, an annual cash award given to six individuals throughout the world who are recognized for their outstanding efforts to advance grass-roots environmental causes. Each of the Goldman Prize winners receive $60,000- by far the most generous international award ever created for environmentalists. Goldman Environmental Prize winners are now an ongoing focus of international publicity.

Richard Goldman understands the importance of timely encouragement. A San Francisco native, Goldman spent a year in law school and four years in the Signal Corps before starting with his own export business. With the urging of close friends, he decided to try his hand at insurance brokering and in 1948, joined friend Herbert Ross to found the insurance brokerage Goldman & Ross. The partnership prospered until 1957, when Richard Goldman elected to start his own firm, Goldman Insurance.

A significant turning point for the young brokerage came in 1960, when Goldman and former president Stuart Seiler bid for the contract to service the San Francisco Unified School District. Faced off against two large insurance companies already serving the district, Goldman assembled a package which included a lower price and consolidated all necessary insurance coverages into one policy. Goldman Insurance was awarded the contract and continues to serve the district today.

The firm has since enjoyed orderly, consistent growth, jealously guarding its independence by refusing numerous buyout offers from national firms. Focusing on its ability to analyze and anticipate the emerging complexities of the insurance brokerage business, Goldman Insurance is planning for its future success and continuity by designating John Goldman, the founder's son, as the comapny's president, and Larry Colton as its executive vice president.

For Richard Goldman, his work—as a professional and as a philanthropist—has been his reward. "I've been able to mix business with community affairs and have a feeling of accomplishment from both. I don't know how you can beat that, but if you can, I'd like to hear it."

Levi Strauss & Co.

QUALITY OF LIFE

Hospitals, universities, and health care organizations serve as the guardians for Bay Area residents by furnishing timely and essential assistance.

▲ Daughters of Charity National Health System ▲ Alta Bates Medical Center
▲ St. Mary's Hospital and Medical Center
▲ Golden Gate University
▲ Ohlone College
▲ Washington Hospital Healthcare Ststem

Photo by Mark E. Gibson

❑ ❑ ❑

203

DAUGHTERS OF CHARITY NATIONAL HEALTH SYSTEM

The Daughters of Charity National Health System (DCNHS), the nation's largest not-for-profit health system, has deep roots in the Bay Area.

Formed in 1986, the St. Louis-based health care system has four regional headquarters, with California and 12 other western states served by the West Region office (DCNHS-West), in the Bay Area city of Los Altos Hills.

What makes DCNHS different? Two core elements within DCNHS combine to make the care provided by its hospitals some of the best available. The first element is the Daughters of Charity, the religious order of women that has been serving the ill and destitute for more than 350 years and continues that tradition at all DCNHS hospitals. The second element is the national health system itself, which oversees the financial and organizational management of nearly 60 DCNHS health care facilities nationwide.

The tradition of service provided by the Daughters of Charity dates back to 1633, when St. Vincent de Paul and St. Louise de Marillac organized the first group of Daughters, the first religious community of women to work among the sick and the poor. Founded and still based in Paris, the order today has more than 34,000 sisters serving the poor, lonely, and afflicted in every part of the world.

In the United States, the Daughters of Charity descended from the Sisters of Charity, a religious community of women established in 1809 in Emmitsburg, Maryland, by Elizabeth Ann Seton, canonized in 1975 as the first American-born saint. In 1850 Mother Seton's community at Emmitsburg was officially united with the Daughters of Charity, today consisting of five United States provinces. The Province of the West, serving 13 western states, is headquartered at the Seton Provincialate in Los Altos Hills. The Daughters of Charity first came to the Bay Area in 1852 when asked to start an orphanage in San Francisco for homeless children of the California gold rush.

Although the Daughters of Charity provide a range of services in three fields—health care, education, and social ministry—the order's focus at DCNHS-West hospitals is on health care services. Today the Daughters are particularly active in the areas of hospital governance, pastoral care for patients, and mission services, in which the Daughters of Charity, through their own example, impart to physicians and staff the spirit and values of their philosophy of service.

The Bay Area settings for the Daughters' health services include some of the region's finest medical facilities: Seton Medical Center in Daly City, St. Catherine Hospital On Half Moon Bay, O'Connor Hospital in San Jose, and Saint Louise Hospital in Morgan Hill.

Located in the geographic center of rapidly growing southern Santa Clara County is the newest of the DCNHS-West hospitals, named for the Daughters of Charity cofounder, Saint Louise. Hospital services in the Morgan Hill area were limited until Saint Louise Hospital opened its doors in October 1989. Its services include 24-hour emergency-room care and an occupational health program that includes pre-placement physicals, drug testing, and CPR training for employers. Prenatal care is provided to women, regardless of their ability to pay, at the Center For Life. Families are welcome to share in the birth of a baby at the Birthing Center in one of five warmly decorated labor-delivery-recovery-postpartum suites. Along with primary care, Saint Louise Hospital is proud of its leading-edge Nuclear Medicine department and freestanding, outpatient Cancer Care Center.

Saint Louise Hospital contributes to the community, initiating programs such as Rotacare to bring needed health care to migrant workers and their families. Associates, physicians, and volunteers work together and contribute to the notable success of this young hospital.

RIGHT: Sister Emily Bourg, D.C., discusses home health care services with a Bay Area resident.

BELOW: Saint Louise Hospital in Morgan Hill.

O'Connor Hospital in San Jose, the first private health care facility in Santa Clara County, is a 398-bed acute-care facility. Founded in 1889 by Judge Myles P. O'Connor, the hospital has undergone several physical transformations, including major expansions, although the services of the Daughters of Charity have remained constant.

In addition to its full complement of general-practice medicine, state-of-the-art maternal/ child health services, cancer care center, Heart Center, and the O'Connor Recovery Center offering inpatient and outpatient treatment of chemical dependency, the hospital has established a multi-site Business Health Network, which provides a link between industry and health care services. Emergency and follow-up care for occupational injuries, physical therapy, pre-employment physicals, work-

site evaluations, preventative medicine, education seminars, and health fairs are among the wide range of health care and wellness programs available through this network.

O'Connor has formed South Bay Health Management Services, Inc., a management services organization, with the O'Connor Medical Group. Three other physician groups, Personal Choice, Montebello, and San Jose Medical Group are affiliated with O'Connor Hospital.

Another of O'Connor's community-outreach success stories is the Senior Circle Program, which provides health service discounts, educational material, and assistance with insurance claims for more than 24,000 senior citizens in Santa Clara County—about 20 percent of the county's senior population.

In their commitment to social responsibility, the Daughters of Charity and O'Connor also participate in a wide range of social-service and community programs, such as the Adopt-a-School Program and Career Academy, which benefit high school students through a variety of internship and scholarship programs.

Some of the Bay Area's best research and development in the area of cardiovascular diseases is done by Seton Medical Center in Daly City, through the San Francisco Heart Institute. Seton was the first Bay Area hospital to perform cardiac angioplasty and continues to be a market leader in cardiology today.

Among other specialized services provided by Seton is family-centered maternity care, which facilitates family participation and support for new mothers, from labor throughdelivery and recovery. The Seton Spine Program, one of the most innovative in the country, is based on a sports-medicine model of care and exercise, and includes a multidisciplinary approach to outpatient treatment. Additionally, Seton's affiliated hospital, St. Catherine Hospital On Half Moon Bay, a 123-bed facility, provides the only emergency and general-medicine services, as well as skilled nursing care, available to coastside residents.

Seton, which has a 357-bed capacity, also works closely with local businesses, insurance companies, and most major health-maintenance and preferred-provider organizations to provide a broad scope of medical and surgical services in a high-quality and cost-effective manner.

Founded in San Francisco in 1893 by the Daughters of Charity, the hospital was originally named Mary's Help Hospital. It was renamed Seton Medical Center in 1983.

The tradition of nearly 150 years of high-quality care while serving the sick poor of the Bay Area continues today. A goal achieved by DCNHS-West hospitals over the past five years is to commit a sum equal to 100 percent of net income for care of the poor and community-benefit services. For 1992, charitable services provided by these hospitals totaled more than $54 million. Charitable services include direct medical care to patients and free or low-cost community outreach programs.

ABOVE: Seton Medical Center in Daly City.

LEFT: O'Connor Hospital in San Jose.

Alta Bates Medical Center

Alta Bates Medical Center enjoys a 170-year history of providing excellent medical care and services to the San Francisco East Bay communities. Alta Bates Medical Center was formed with the merger of two separate hospitals in 1988, Alta Bates Hospital and Herrick Hospital and Health Center. These two facilities opened in Berkeley just after the turn of the century in response to the community's medical needs resulting from citizens migrating from that era's catastrophic earthquake and fires.

In 1905 at the age of 25, nurse Alta Alice Miner Bates opened an eight-bed sanitarium for women and children, providing the roots for one of the Bay Area's most renowned maternity programs, now delivering more than 3,500 babies a year.

Herrick Hospital, founded by Dr. Leroy Herrick, first opened in 1904 as Roosevelt Hospital, offering the first psychiatric inpatient services in the East Bay. Today these two programs, psychiatry and obstetrics, are regionally recognized and remain integral parts of the medical center's array of services and programs. As the hospital grew in size, the scope of its medical technology and delivery of health care grew to meet the increasing demands of the patients and families served.

Over the years, Alta Bates Medical Center has paid particular attention to developing specialty programs and services which meet the varied needs of community residents. Many are regional in nature and include the following:

• The Bay Area's first comprehensive bone marrow transplantation program—now having treated over 80 patients—allowing patients and their families to stay in the Bay Area rather than travelling great distances.

• A regionally recognized burn center. Now in its 15th year, the Burn Center and the entire medical center responded to it's community during the disasterous 1991 Oakland/Berkeley fire.

• Alta Bates Medical Center's High-Risk Obstetrics Program was the first program in the East Bay designed to manage pregnancies that have added complications such as diabetes, hypertension, heart disease, or high risk of premature labor. The In Vitro Fertilization Program is ranked among the top ten in the nation—assisting childless couples in their quest for their own baby.

• The Center's Hospice program is offered through it's Visiting Nurse Association. Hospice is a 24-hour interdisciplinary service for terminally ill patients and their families. Geared specifically for those who wish to die at home,

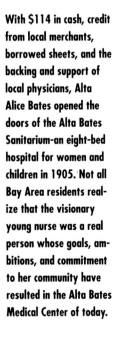

With $114 in cash, credit from local merchants, borrowed sheets, and the backing and support of local physicians, Alta Alice Bates opened the doors of the Alta Bates Sanitarium-an eight-bed hospital for women and children in 1905. Not all Bay Area residents realize that the visionary young nurse was a real person whose goals, ambitions, and commitment to her community have resulted in the Alta Bates Medical Center of today.

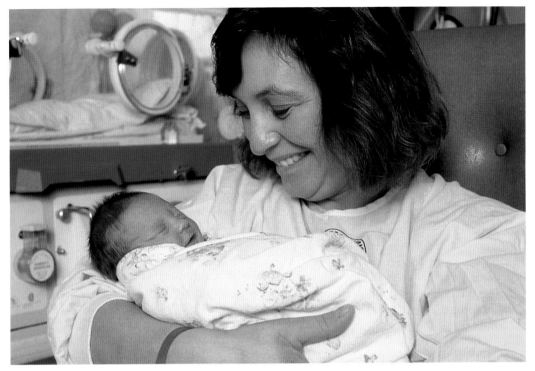

Having received the distinct honor as the hospital offering the best care for newborns in the state, Alta Bates Medical Center takes great pride in its Women and Infant Services. Delivering 4,000 babies a year, the hospital has been a leader in high-risk obstetrics, in vitro fertilization, parent education, and neonatal intensive care. Plans for a new era in the delivery of women's health care will be realized with the completition of the hospital's new women's pavilion, representing the most progressive approach to the care of women and infants in the nation. Photo by Ken Lee.

Hospice includes intermittent nursing care, symptom management, respite care for family members, counseling, spirtual support, and bereavement counseling.

•A free 'round-the-clock community service project is the innovative Ask-A-Nurse program. Staffed by registered nurses, the information line helps individuals decide the best course of action with immediate medical questions.

Additionally, the Alta Bates takes great pride in an adult sickle cell program, older adult services, stroke and head injury rehabilitation, cardiovascular services, and the East Bay AIDS Center. These programs further complement state-of-the-art treatment closer to home and services which meet the changing health care needs of the community.

Today this tertiary, acute care medical center operates 500 beds, including a 30-bed hospital-based skilled nursing facility. The lifeblood of all these services, of course, is the doctors and staff who provide them. Nine hundred physicians and more than 2,530 full-time, part-time, and on-call staffers serve the center's patients. In managing this huge staff, Alta Bates Medical Center's president and CEO, Albert Greene, is clear about his priorities: The lines of communication among management, physicians, support staff, and the community, he believes, are as important as the hospital's medical technology.

"In 17 years as a hospital administrator, I never once received a letter from a patient saying a machine did a great job," Greene said in 1990, shortly after leaving Sinai Samaritan Medical Center in Milwaukee to join Alta Bates. "Only people do great jobs, and people do great jobs when they're comfortable. My goal is for the overwhelming majority of employees to say that they work for Alta Bates Medical Center, as part of a team. To achieve that communication and commitment is essential."

Greene's people-oriented approach takes on additional importance as the hospital continues to improve and expand its facilities and services. As always, Alta Bates is developing and refining helath care services consistent with its history, by responding to the Bay Area community. New services and programs can be seen in the cardiac cath lab, a new Vascular Center, and remoldeling of the highly respected Labor and Delivery areas. Construction is planned at the Dwight Way Site for a 24-hours-a-day, seven-days-a-week Comprehensive Cancer Center.

Whether seasoned with years of history or recently initiated, each program offers the same commitment to quality, compassionate care that is the hallmark of Alta Bates Medical Center.

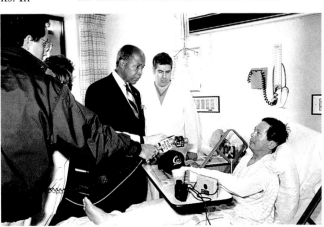

Members of the media follow the honorable Louis W. Sullivan, M.D., U.S. Secretary of Health and Human Services, on his tour of the Alta Bates Burn Center following the October 20, 1991, Oakland/Berkeley firestorm. In addition to six burn patients admitted to its regional burn center, Alta Bates treated 50 patients in its Emergency Department in the first 24 hours of the fire. Photo by Ken Lee.

ST. MARY'S HOSPITAL AND MEDICAL CENTER

Today's St. Mary's Hospital and Medical Center is a descendant of San Francisco's first and most famous private health care institution.

The founders of the hospital were the Sisters of Mercy, a Catholic order of women that in 1854 called upon eight of its members to bring mercy to the shores of San Francisco. After a treacherous ocean voyage, the Sisters arrived in San Francisco to find it in the grip of gold rush fever and a deadly cholera epidemic.

The Sisters immediately began caring for the sick at the State Marine and County Hospital at Stockton Street and Broadway. Although the epidemic passed, the Sisters' tradition of compassionate care in San Francisco had just begun.

In 1857 the Sisters purchased the state facility and named it St. Mary's Hospital, thereby launching the first Catholic hospital on the Pacific coast. In 1861 a new, larger St. Mary's was built on Rincon Hill, which remained the Sisters' base of operations—and one of the city's main health care resources—until it was destroyed in a fire caused by the 1906 earthquake.

But the Sisters were undaunted even by the quake. St. Mary's set up temporary hospital facilities in a tent camp adjacent to Golden Gate Park. In 1911 the hospital once again opened its doors, this time at its present site at Hayes and Stanyan streets.

Today the hospital has 531 licensed beds and a staff that includes more than 700 physicians and 1,400 health care professionals. The staff is backed by the finest medical technology, including a newly installed magnetic resonance imaging machine, which provides the most detailed diagnostic imaging available.

St. Mary's offers particular expertise in orthopedics, rehabilitation, psychiatry, and cardiology. The Western Heart Institute, for example, is responsible for major breakthroughs in clinical heart care and cardiovascular research, including bypass procedures and balloon angioplasty. The McAuley Neuropsychiatric Institute provides all levels of mental health care, from inpatient therapy to day-treatment programs to outpatient services for adults, adolescents, and children. St. Mary's Spine Center is one of the first facilities in the United States dedicated to the diagnosis and treatment of back problems. St. Mary's Rehabilitation Center provides comprehensive services for injured or debilitated patients, including those with spinal cord injuries, traumatic head injuries, and strokes.

But St. Mary's also is a full-service health care organization providing a comprehensive range of medical care services, including services such as chemical dependency, physical medicine, spine care, weight management, mammography, and occupational medicine.

Each year, St. Mary's treats more than 10,000 inpatients and handles more than 12,000 emergency cases. Annual gross revenues exceed $200 million. These numbers are sustained year after year not only by the hospital's reputation for medical excellence but by its sensitivity to the city's cultural diversity.

St. Mary's is a descendant of San Francisco's first and most famous private health care institution.

LEFT: Each year, the hospital treats more than 10,000 inpatients and handles more than 12,000 emergency cases.

"The ethnicity of San Francisco has changed dramatically since the early 1980s," says St. Mary's marketing director Alan Tomiyama, noting increases in the city's Latin American and Asian immigrant populations. "We really have to be at the forefront in meeting those patients' needs, too."

Another area of focus: San Francisco's senior citizens. St. Mary's Senior Life Services is among the most comprehensive and multidisciplinary programs anywhere, offering everything from specialized inpatient care to adult day care, a comprehensive outpatient rehabilitation program, and social programs for older adults.

In 1991 St. Mary's completed construction of The Carlisle at 1450 Post Street, a condominium high rise with more than 100 units that is open to persons 65 and older. The project is designed to help seniors in good health stay that way. To that end, the project includes such on-site amenities as health classes, physician and nursing services, and the services of talented gourmet chefs. Owner-residents at the project also have immediate access to St. Mary's hospital. "It provides a high

level of security and comfort for a growing but underserved segment of the community," observes Tomiyama.

In the field of occupational medicine, St. Mary's has developed some of the Bay Area's most effective illness prevention and treatment programs geared toward helping employers control their health care costs. Everything from basic diagnostic services to hospital care is administered with attention to efficiency and cost. When hospital care is required, Tomiyama adds, "our medical and support staffs try to work toward getting employees back to their jobs as quickly as possible, and in the best of health."

Today St. Mary's has 531 licensed beds and a staff of more than 700 physicians and 1,400 health care professionals.

Golden Gate University

In 1853 attorney William K. Osborn founded the YMCA in San Francisco as a refuge from the social chaos that dominated the city during the gold rush era. What Osborn couldn't have imagined, despite the YMCA's popularity in the late 1800s, was that his refuge would evolve into Golden Gate University, one of the Bay Area's finest institutions for professional education.

Beginning with a simple library and lecture hall, the YMCA launched its first informal academic program in 1881: the YMCA Night School, later renamed the YMCA Evening College. The Evening College gave rise in 1901 to the officially recognized forerunner of Golden

Day and night at Golden Gate University's main campus in downtown San Francisco.

Gate University, the YMCA law school, which offered a formal curriculum leading to an academic degree.

The law school operates today as the Golden Gate University School of Law, one of several undergraduate and graduate programs that the university provides for men and women in business, public service, and law.

Of the school's approximately 7,500 students, about 40 percent are MBA candidates. In fact, each year Golden Gate graduates more MBAs than any other school in Northern California. Alumni include some of the Bay Area's best-known business leaders. One of the school's most prominent MBA graduates is Bank of America chief executive officer Richard Rosenberg, who also earned a law degree from Golden Gate.

Reflecting the growing demand for high-quality business education in Northern California, Golden Gate has consolidated most of its off-campus locations, which formerly included 30 programs throughout the country, to 10 locations in the greater Bay Area. While some of these locations are military bases, most Golden Gate programs are offered in such Bay Area towns as Los Altos, Walnut Creek, Sacramento, and Monterey.

Golden Gate has developed a wide range of study specialties leading to the MBA degree, including finance, marketing, public administration, information systems, telecommunications, international affairs, and health services.

And for managers and professionals with a minimum of five years' professional experience, Golden Gate provides an executive MBA program that focuses on finance, human resources, organizational behavior, marketing, and operations.

To further accommodate the professional and scheduling needs of its students, the university conducts three, 15-week terms each year, enabling students to make uninterrupted progress toward their academic goals. In addition, the university offers 12-week terms and intensive programs that meet on Fridays and Saturdays.

Whatever field of study they choose, Golden Gate students are assured of getting the best instruction available. The university has established industry advisory committees that draw on the expertise of the nation's top professionals to refine the curriculum and keep it current. What's more, Golden Gate is committed to maintaining working relationships with business and government organizations—a commitment in keeping with the university's status as a Bay Area pioneer in higher education.

OHLONE COLLEGE

O hlone College, the centerpiece of the Fremont-Newark Community College District, celebrates its 26th anniversary during the 1992-1993 school year. Ohlone has been providing students with quality academic instruction, career training, personal development, and cultural enrichment opportunities since 1967.

The Fremont-Newark Community College District, which was voted into existence in 1965, officially named the college after the Ohlone Indians who once inhabited the area. Ohlone conducted classes at the former Serra Center Home for Girls in Fremont from 1967 until 1974, when the permanent 534-acre main campus opened on the Huddleson Ranch property in the Mission San Jose foothills. This unique setting offers panoramic views of the metropolitan Bay Area in a rural environment of ponds, palms, and rolling hills.

The college offers over 30 occupational programs and academic majors in more than 45 areas. For students intending to transfer, most academic course credits from Ohlone are accepted at the state's four-year institutions and many independent universities. Accredited by the Western Association of Schools and Colleges since 1970, Ohlone awards Associate in Arts or Associate in Science degrees to students who successfully complete 60 or more semester units in appropriate major-field and general-requirement courses. As a supplement to these instructional programs, the college provides a comprehensive range of student activities, and educational and career counseling services.

In addition to its academic curriculum,

Ohlone's Community Services office offers non-credit, fee-supported seminars in business and personal development. In partnership with the local business community, Ohlone has also established a worksite training program for the employees of local businesses.

Along with quality instruction and the diversity of its programs, Ohlone has made accessibility to education its top priority. For registered students who find it difficult to attend classes on campus, for example, Ohlone offers a unique approach to education: college courses on the radio. Lectures broadcast over the college station, KOHL-FM (89.3), have been particularly helpful for people with disabilities and senior students, allowing them to tape courses for later listening and review. Additionally, Ohlone holds classes in seven off-campus locations.

Ohlone also provides some of Northern California's finest educational programs for deaf students. The main campus includes the Ohlone College Center for the Deaf and is also the site of the Gallaudet Regional Center—one of seven extension facilities of Gallaudet University College of Continuing Education, based in Washington, D.C. This regional center provides continuing community education as well as information and resources on deaf-related issues.

As Ohlone enters its second quarter-century, the college renews its commitment to providing students with the skills they will need to function effectively in a changing world. Ohlone balances innovation with tradition by offering up-to-date curriculum that keeps pace with the changes in technological fields and by promoting values that reflect a commitment to the human touch.

WASHINGTON HOSPITAL HEALTHCARE SYSTEM

Washington Hospital Healthcare System, a public hospital district, serves a portion of what southern Alameda County WHHS staffers like to call "Washington Country."

Washington Country's extensive range of services and facilities started with the opening of a single, 150-bed facility, Washington Hospital. Opened in November 1958, that hospital has evolved into a health care system that now serves Fremont, Newark, Union City, and part of south Hayward—a district of approximately 124 square miles and 265,000 residents.

Two things perpetuated Washington Hospital's growth into WHHS: the growth of Alameda County and the hospital's commitment to providing high-quality health care with state-of-the-art medical technology and training. Washington Hospital's transformation alone is remarkable. A six-story wing constructed in 1974 transformed the facility into a full-service acute-care general hospital with 265 beds. The addition of a fifth-floor nursing unit in 1990 increased the hospital's bed capacity to 305.

WHHS also includes five clinics: the Washington Stanford Radiation Oncology Center, the Washington Outpatient Surgery Center, the Washington Outpatient Rehabilitation Center, the Washington Birthing Center, and the Washington Heart Institute.

Washington Township Hospital District is governed through a publicly elected five-member board of directors. More than 300 physicians and 1,400 staffers keep these facilities running at peak performance, providing patients with the kind of caring service that has become a WHHS signature.

Indeed, for WHHS board members, physicians, volunteers, and staffers, the real milestones of Washington's history are those times when the care and skills of medical professionals save and improve lives.

In 1985, 70 schoolchildren were treated at Washington following a fatal accident involving their school bus. Just before Christmas in 1987, a newborn infant was found abandoned in a Fremont gas station; Washington Hospital nurses cared for her and nicknamed her Holly Noelle Washington. In 1992 baby number 1,000 was born at the Washington Birthing Center. In that same year, more than 2,500 babies were born in the WHHS.

By Washington Hospital Healthcare System standards, saving and prolonging lives are the truly significant events in Washington Country.

Washington Hospital Healthcare System in Fremont, California, is a 305-bed acute-care general hospital serving the people of Fremont, Newark, Union City, and part of south Hayward.

DIRECTORY OF CORPORATE SPONSORS